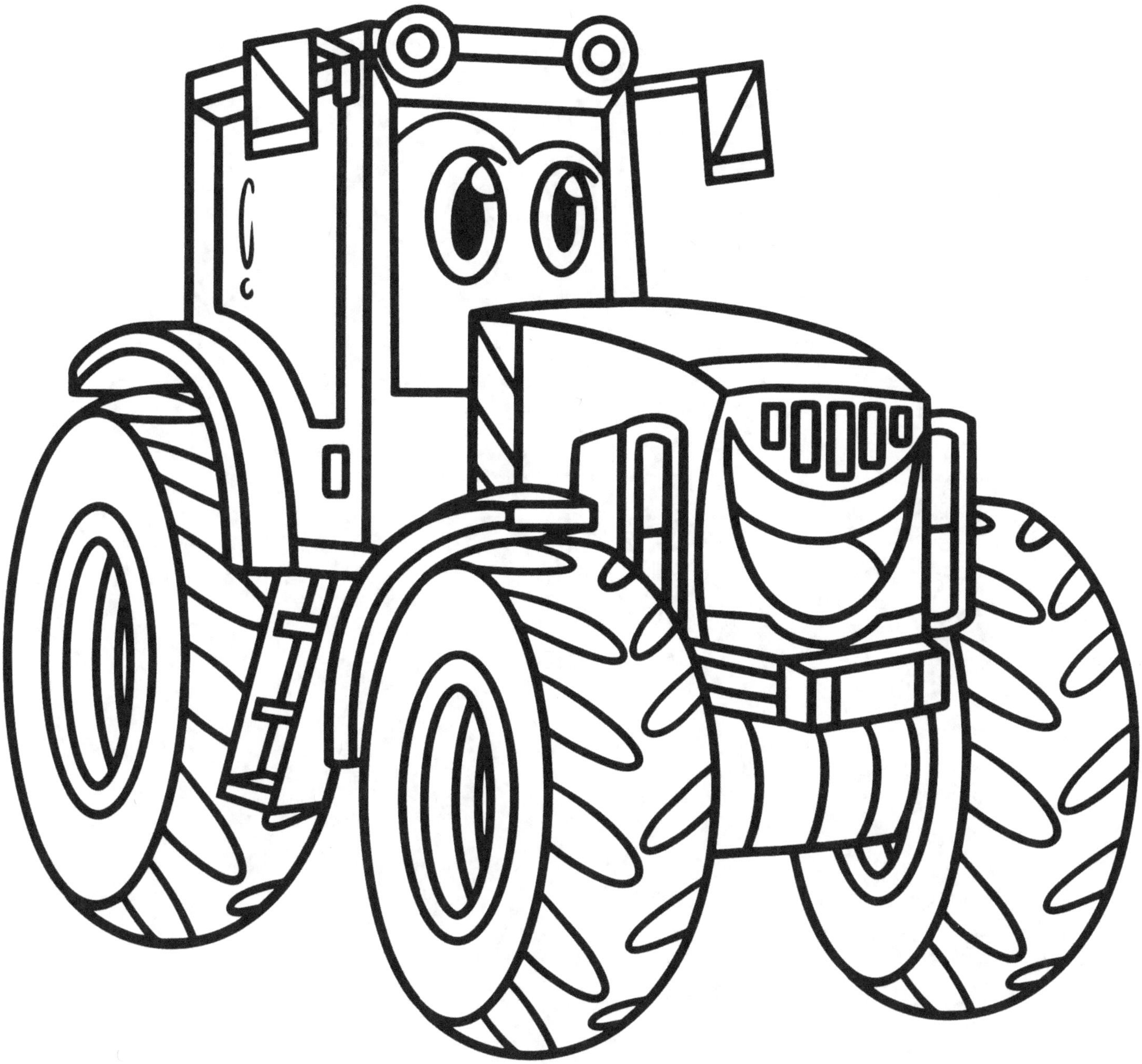

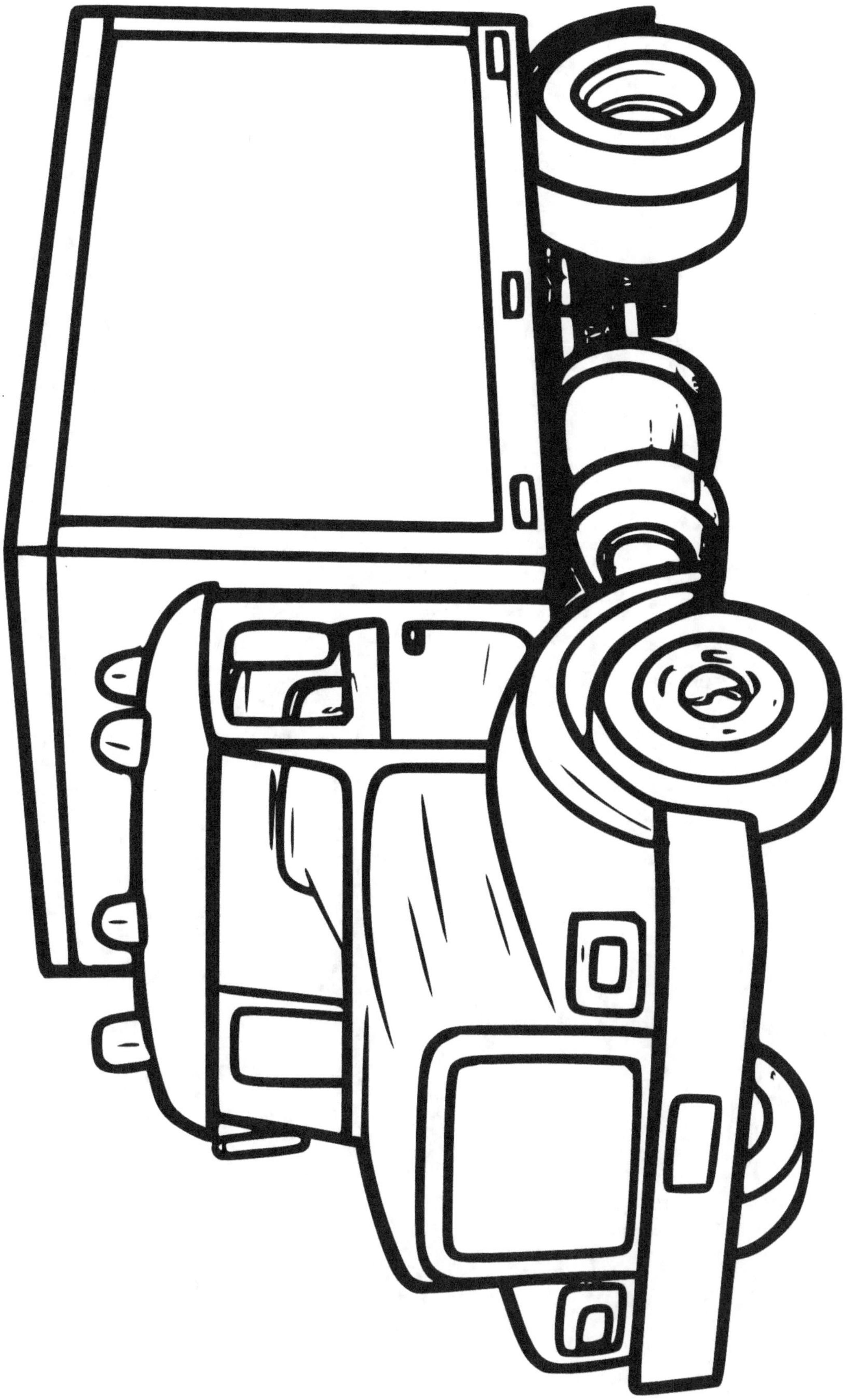

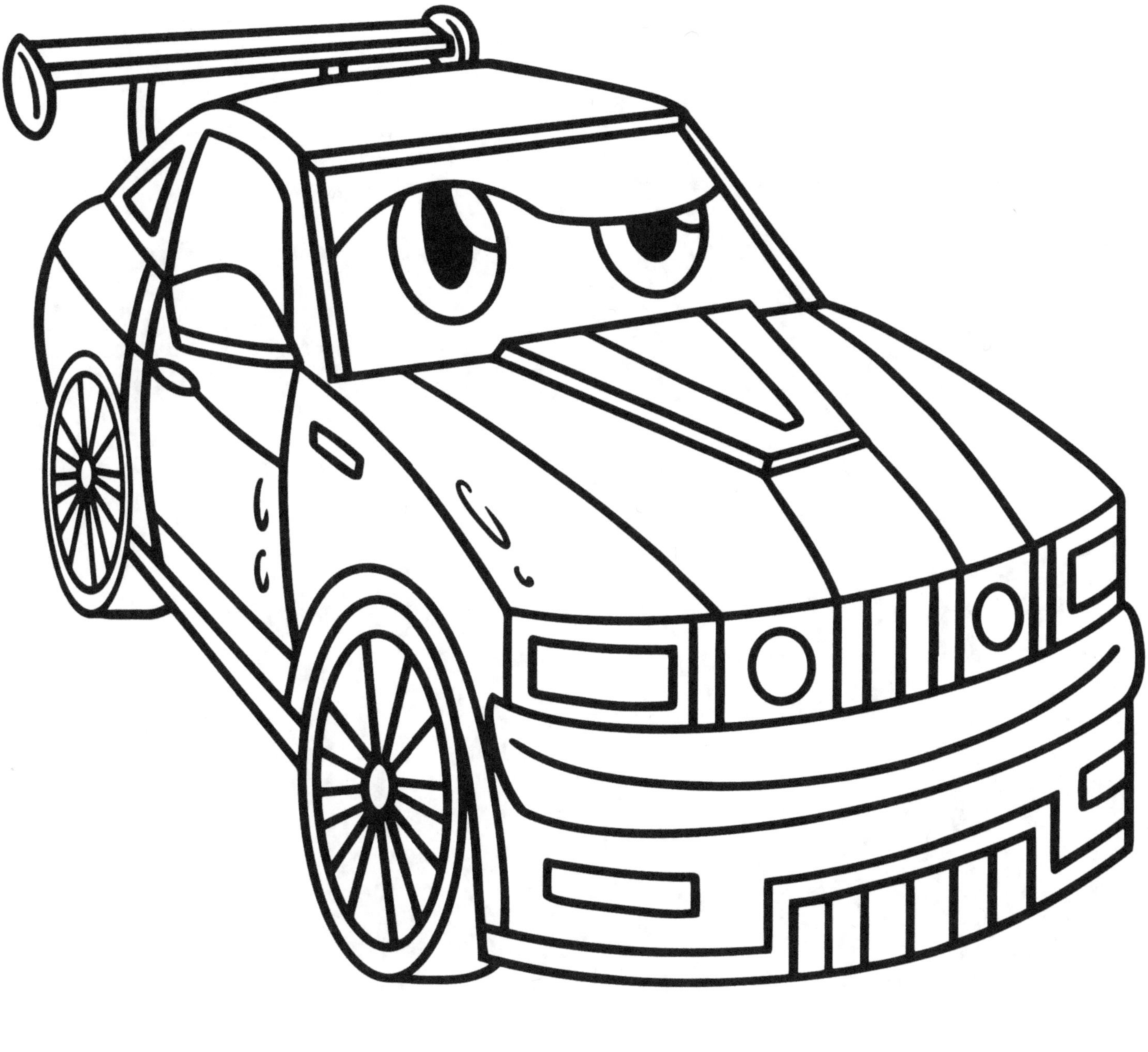

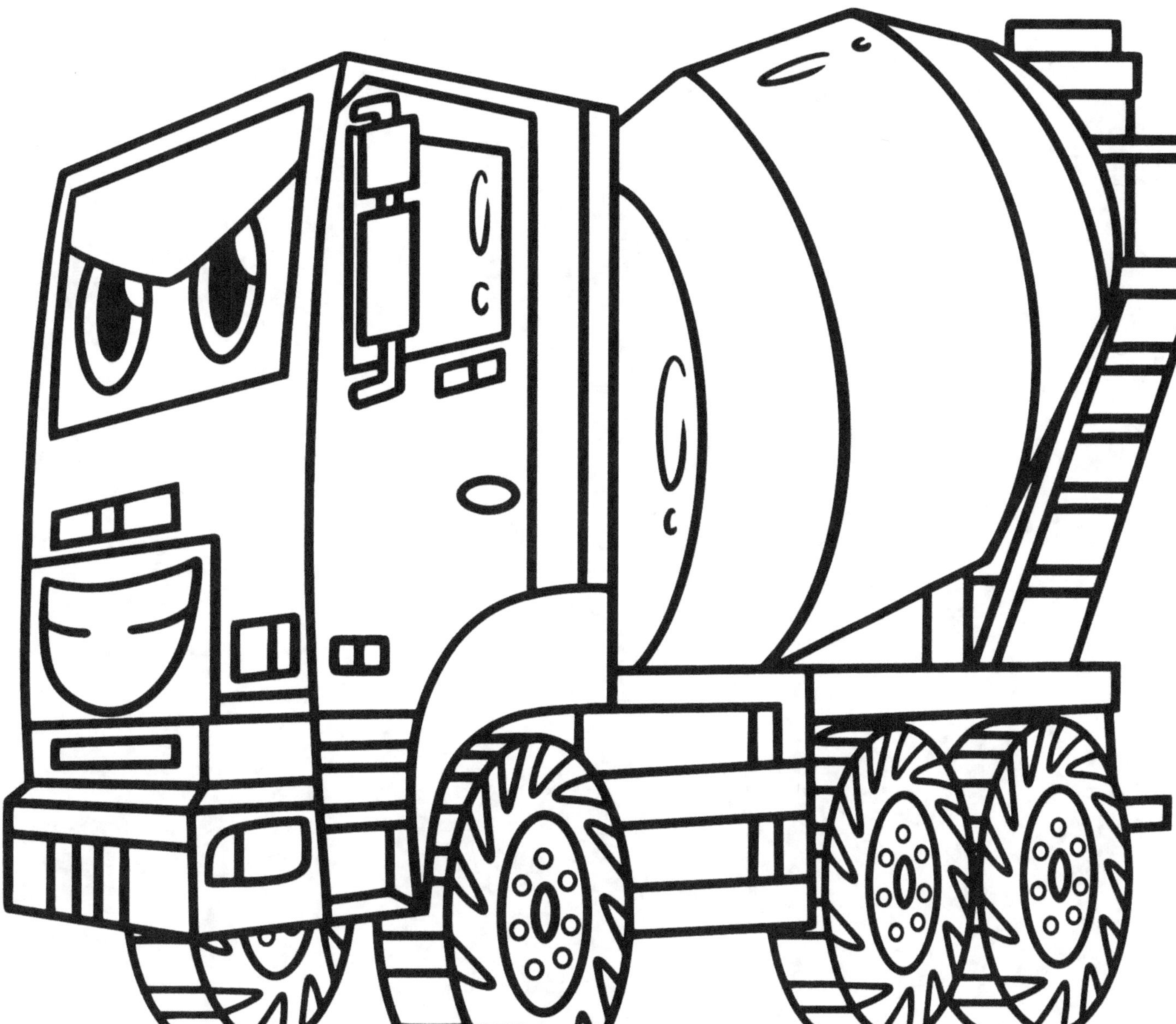

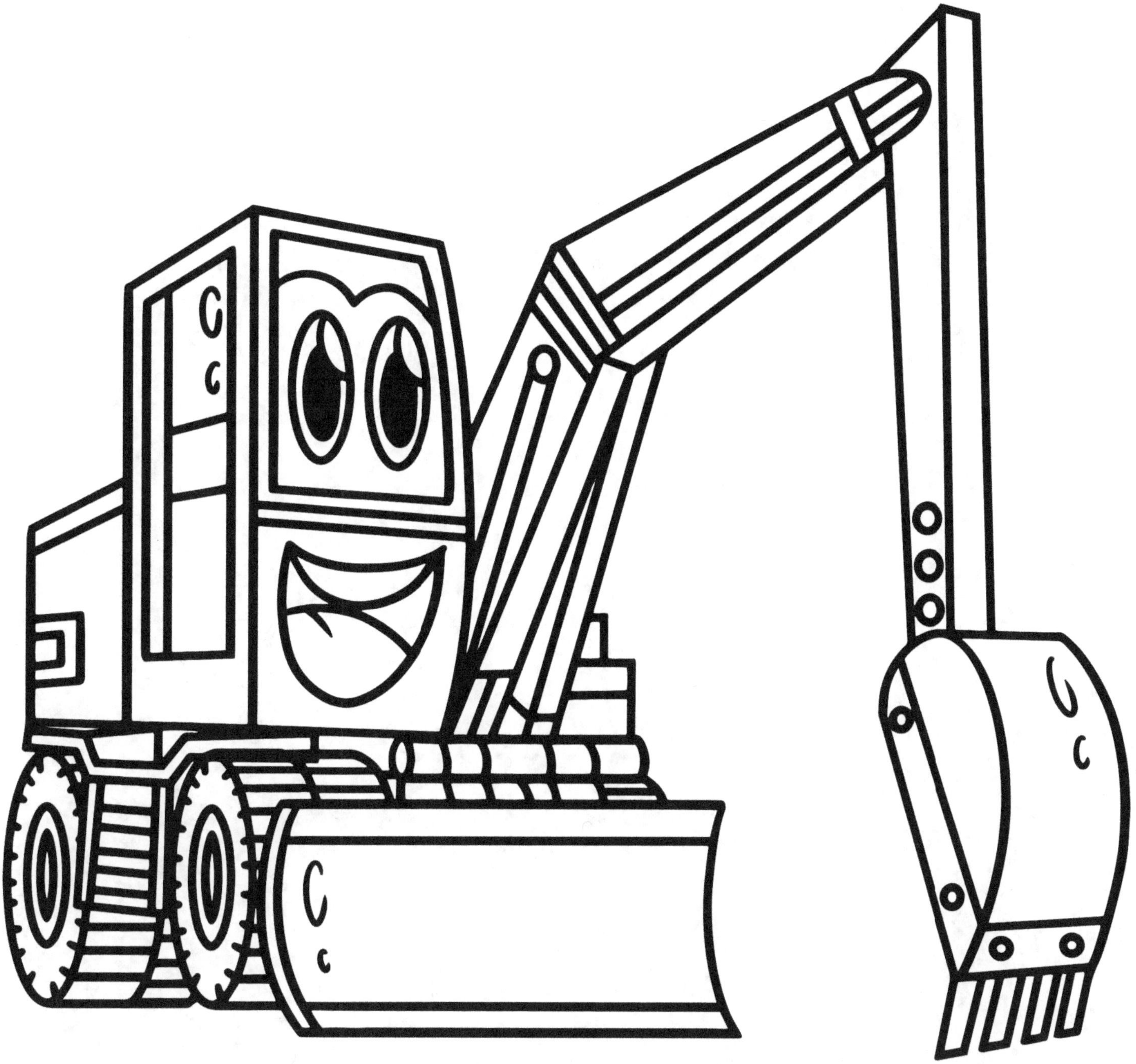

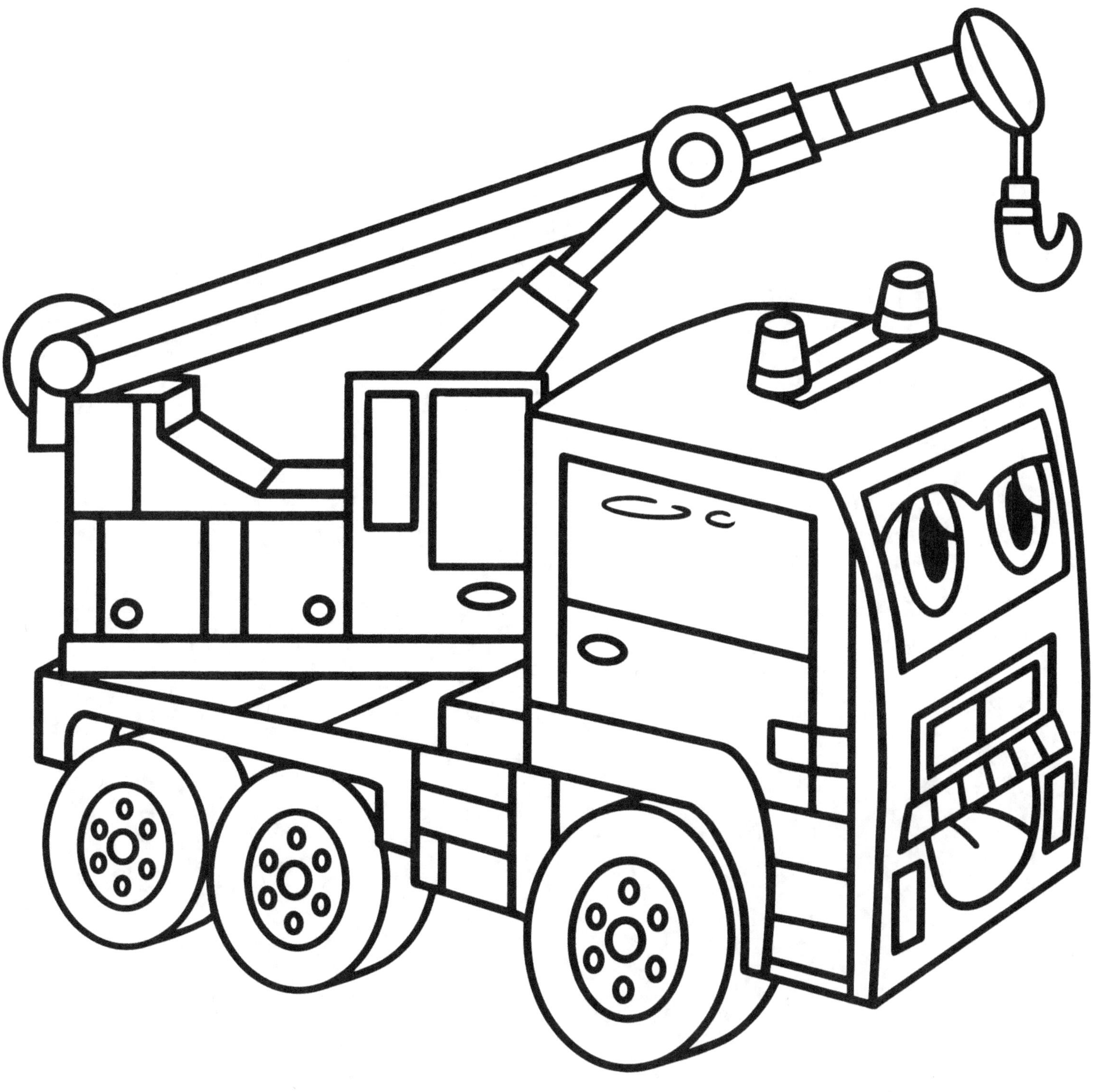

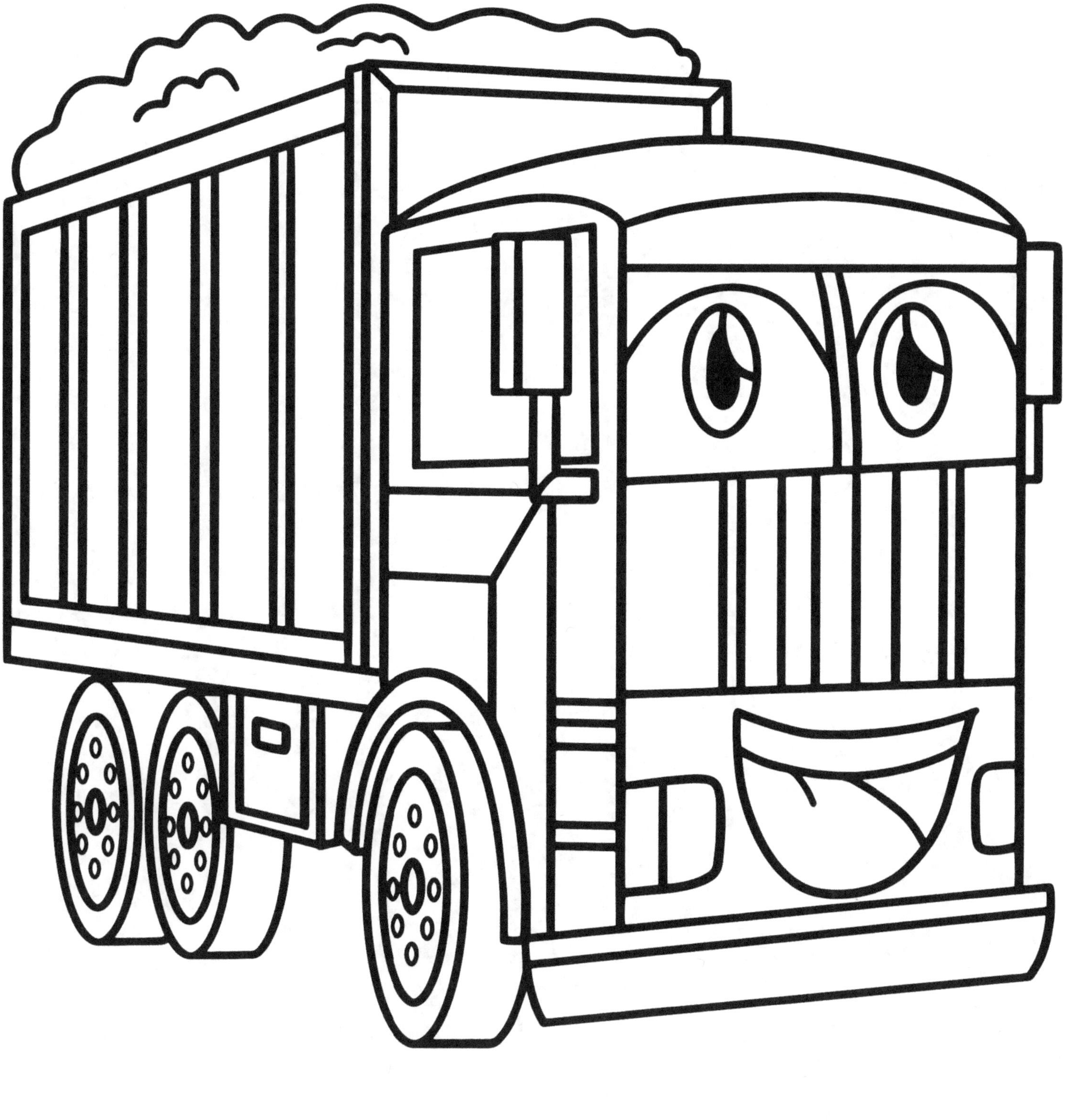

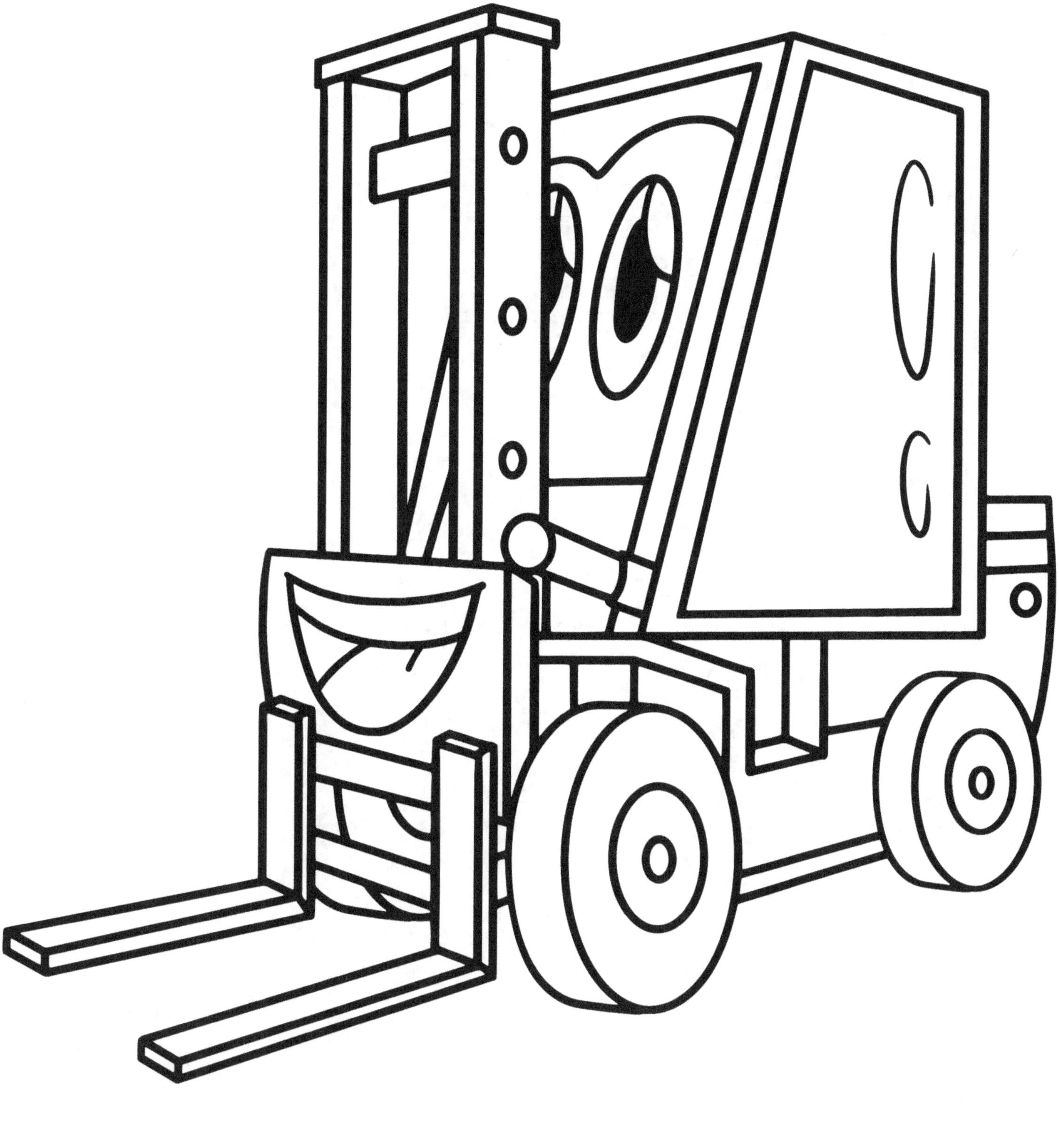

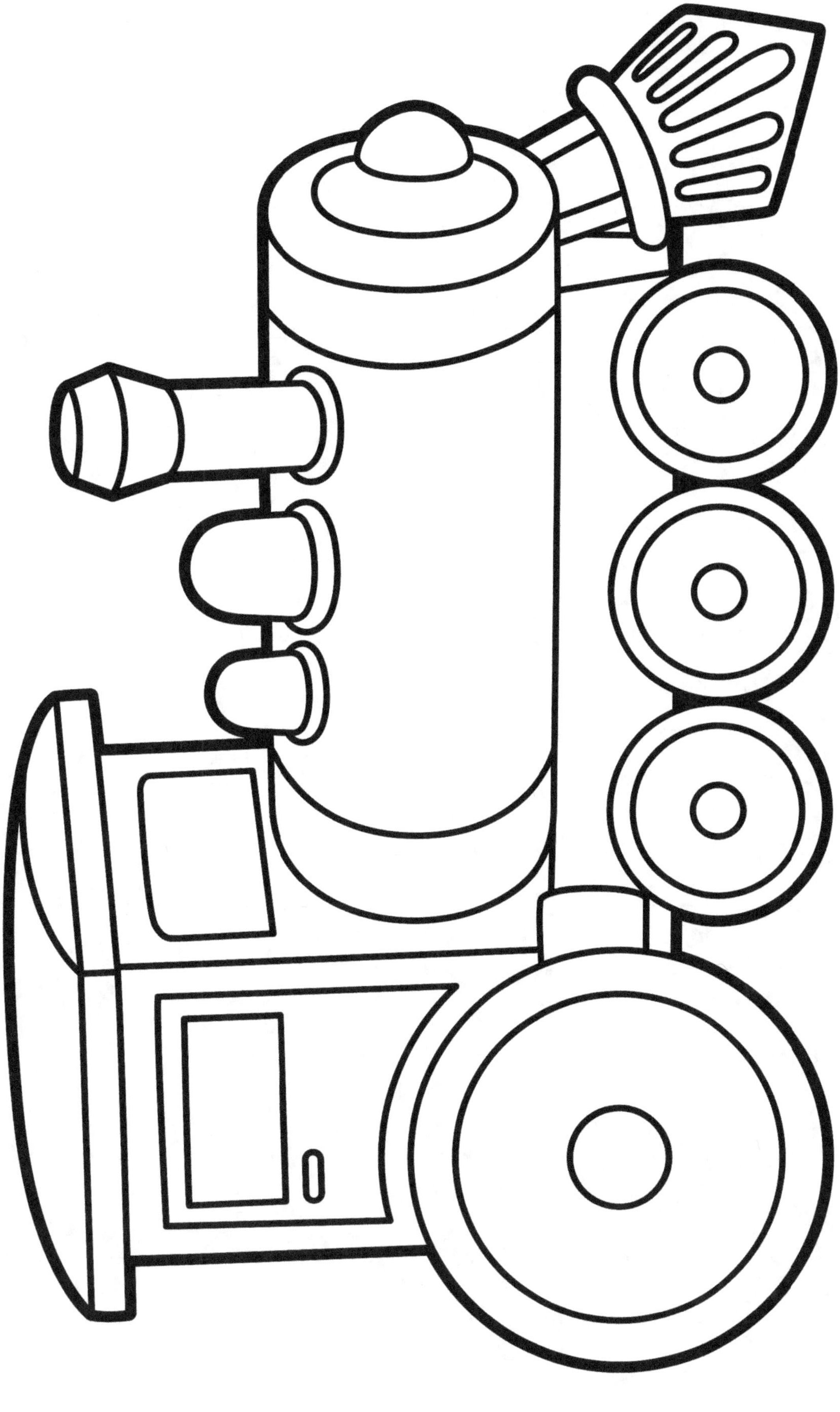

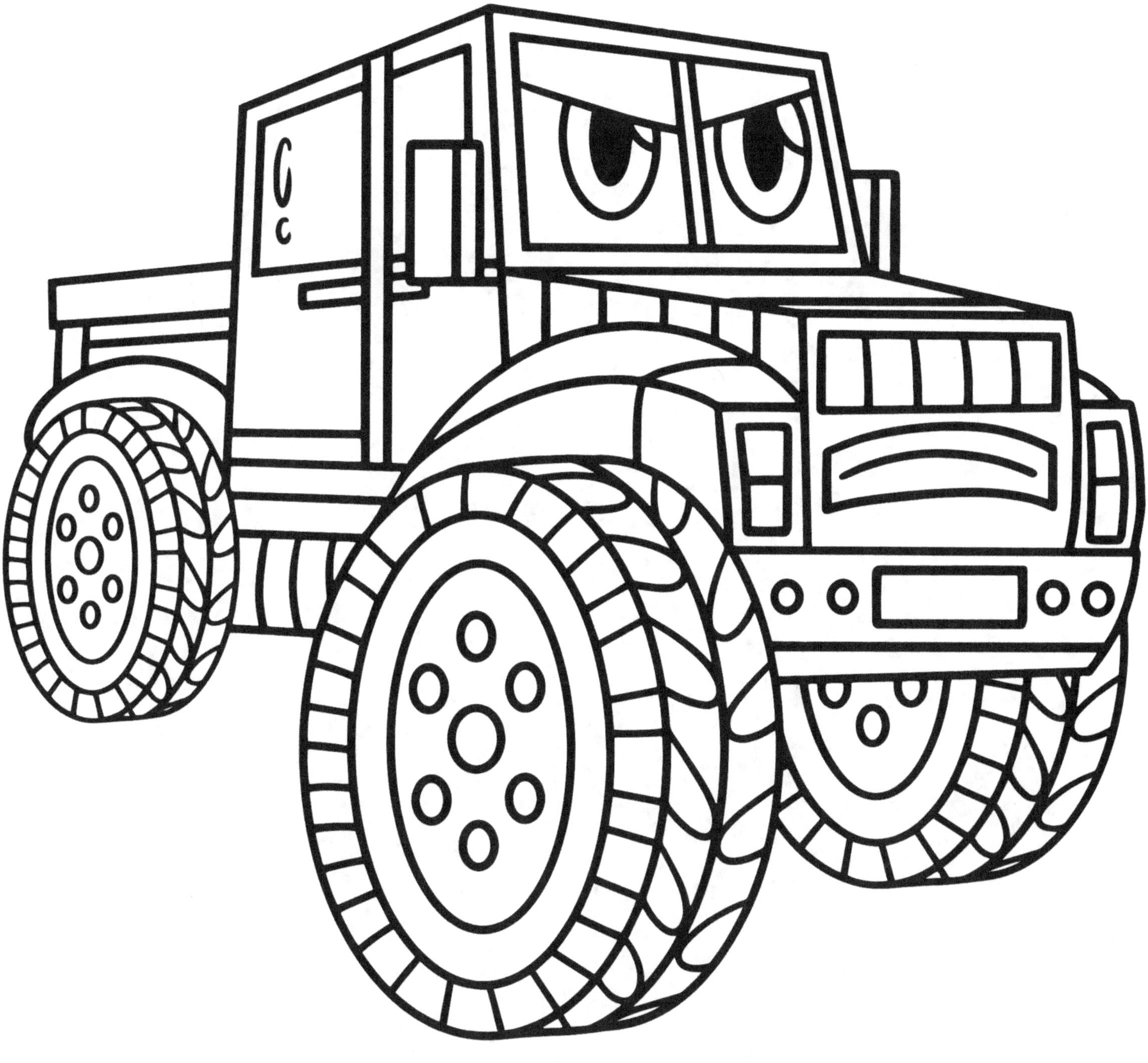

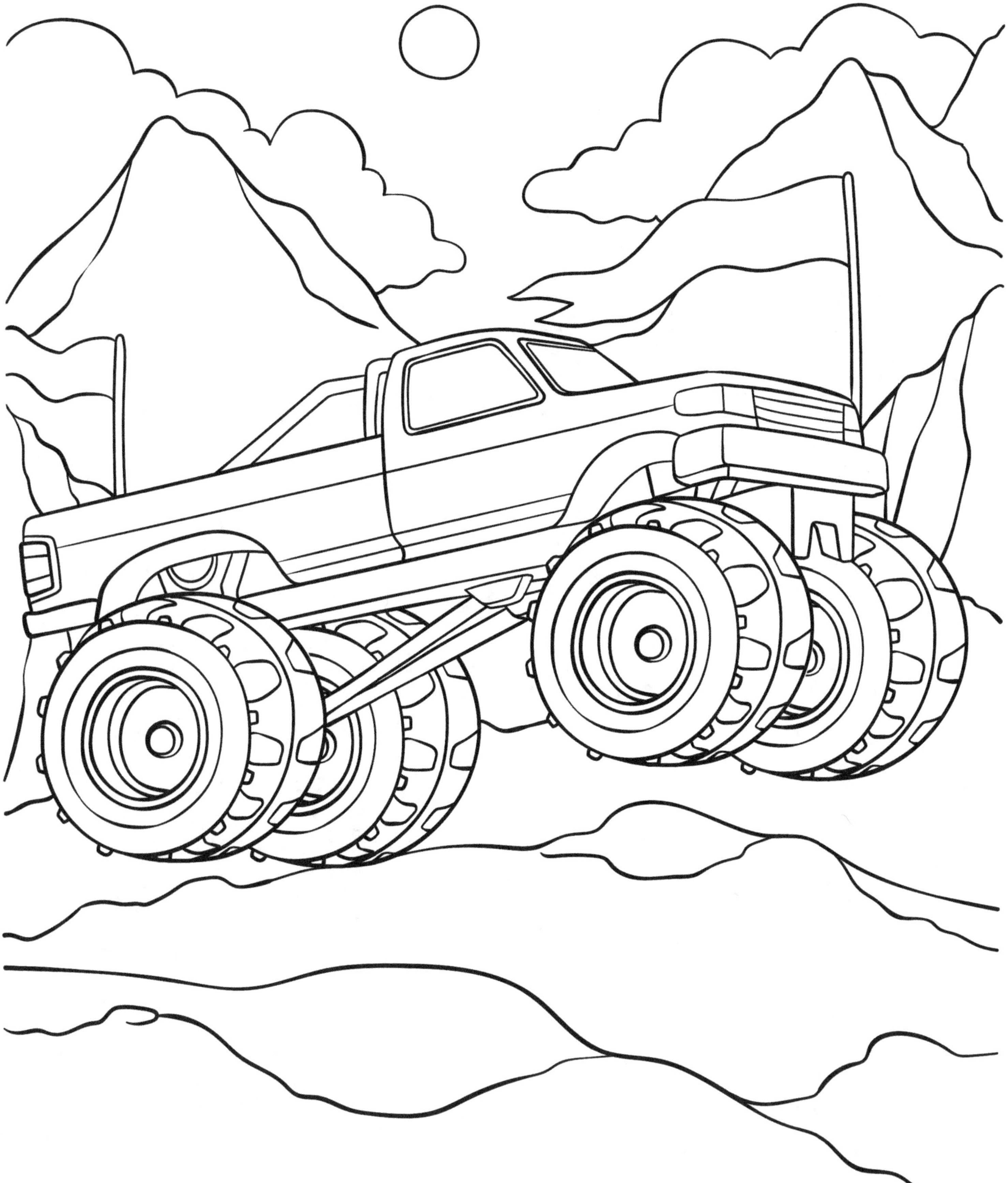

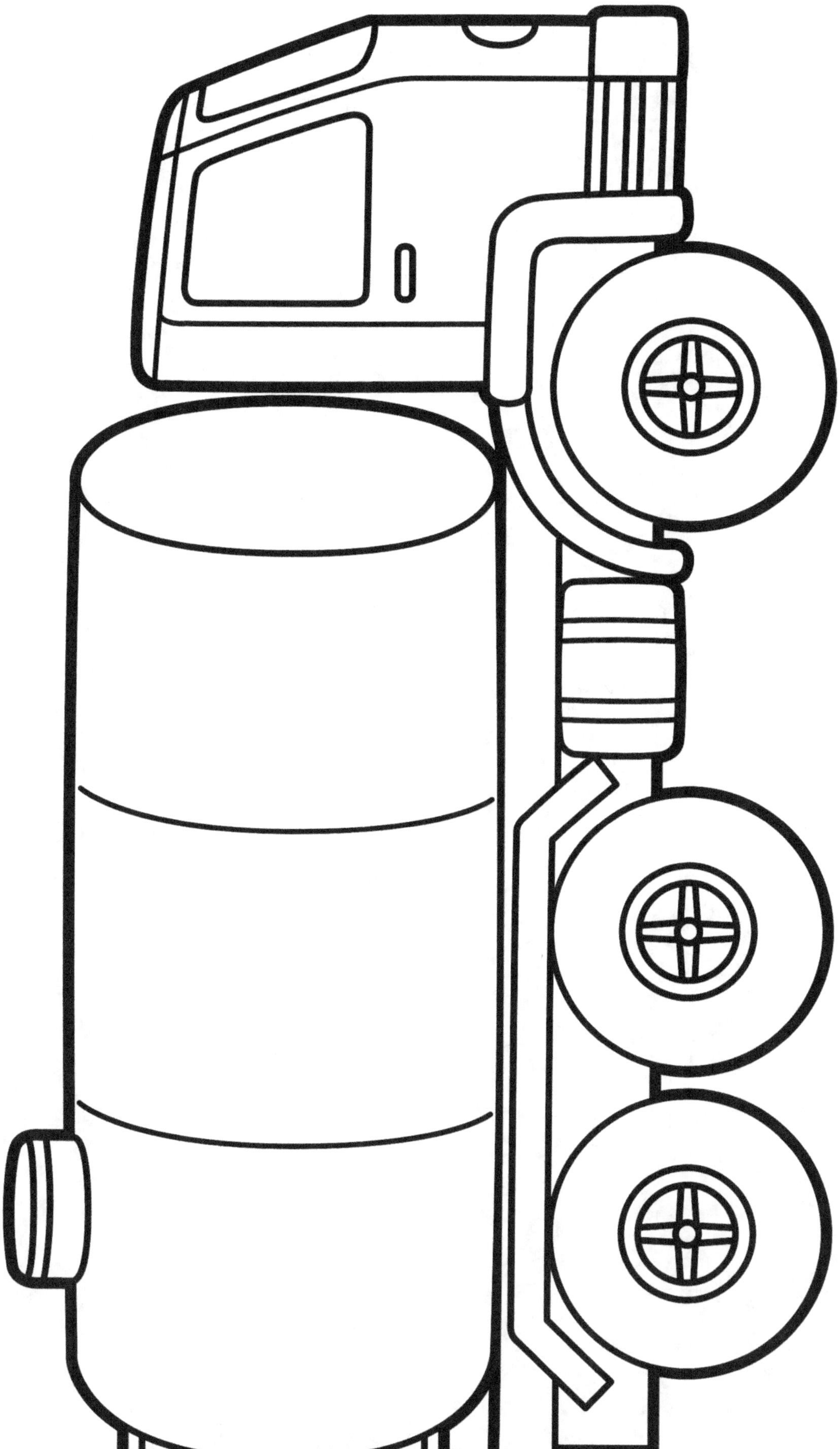

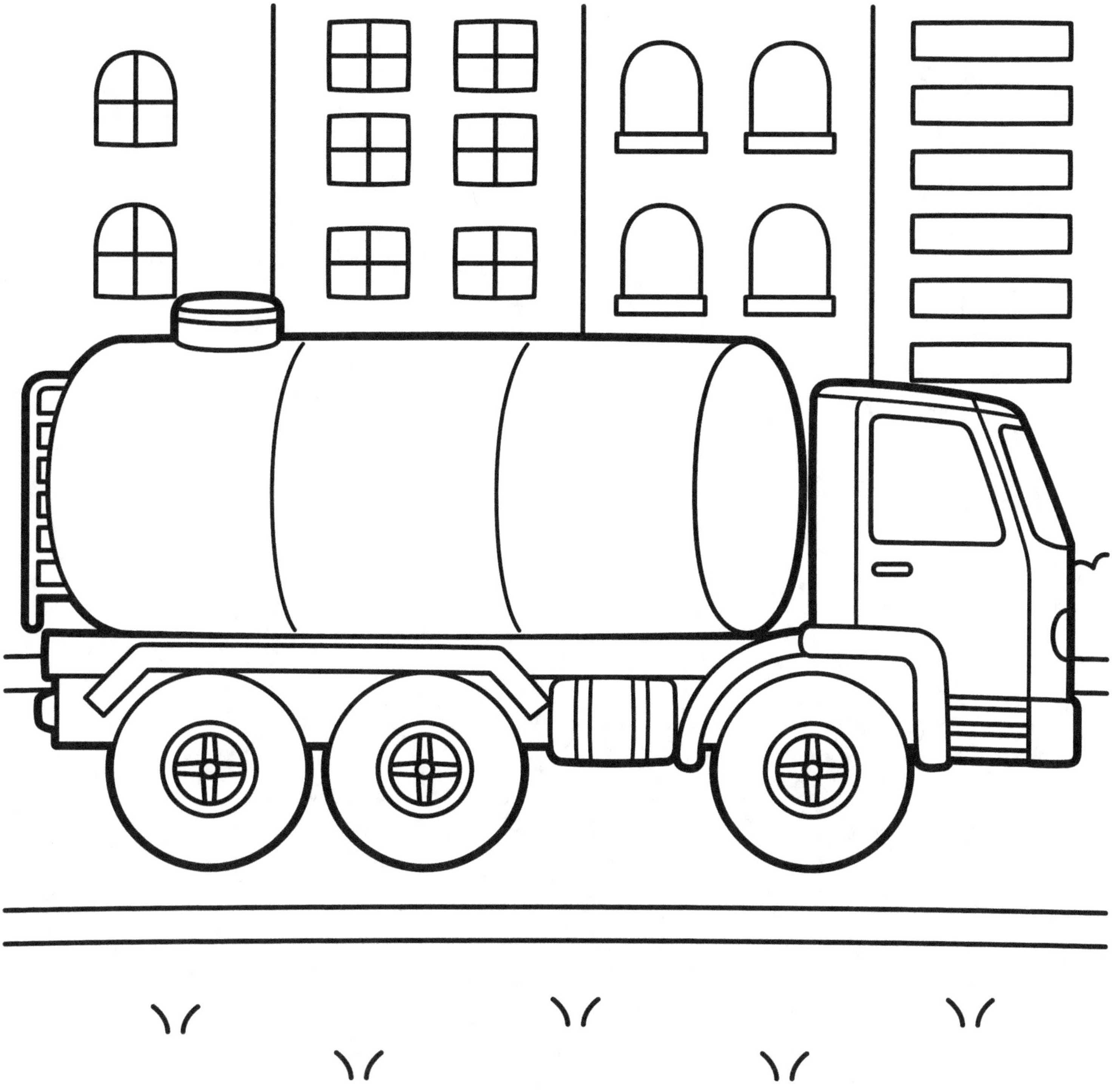

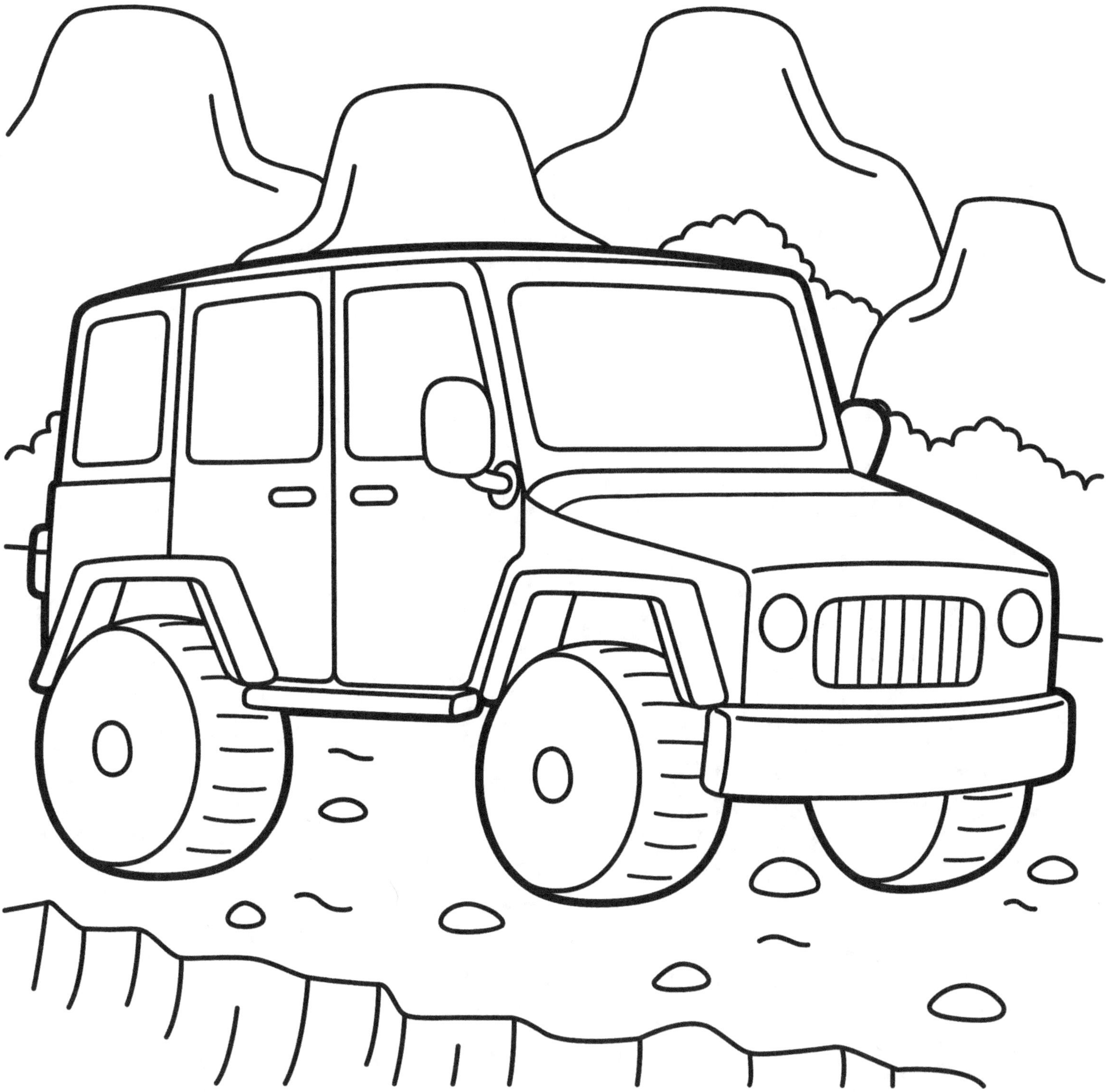

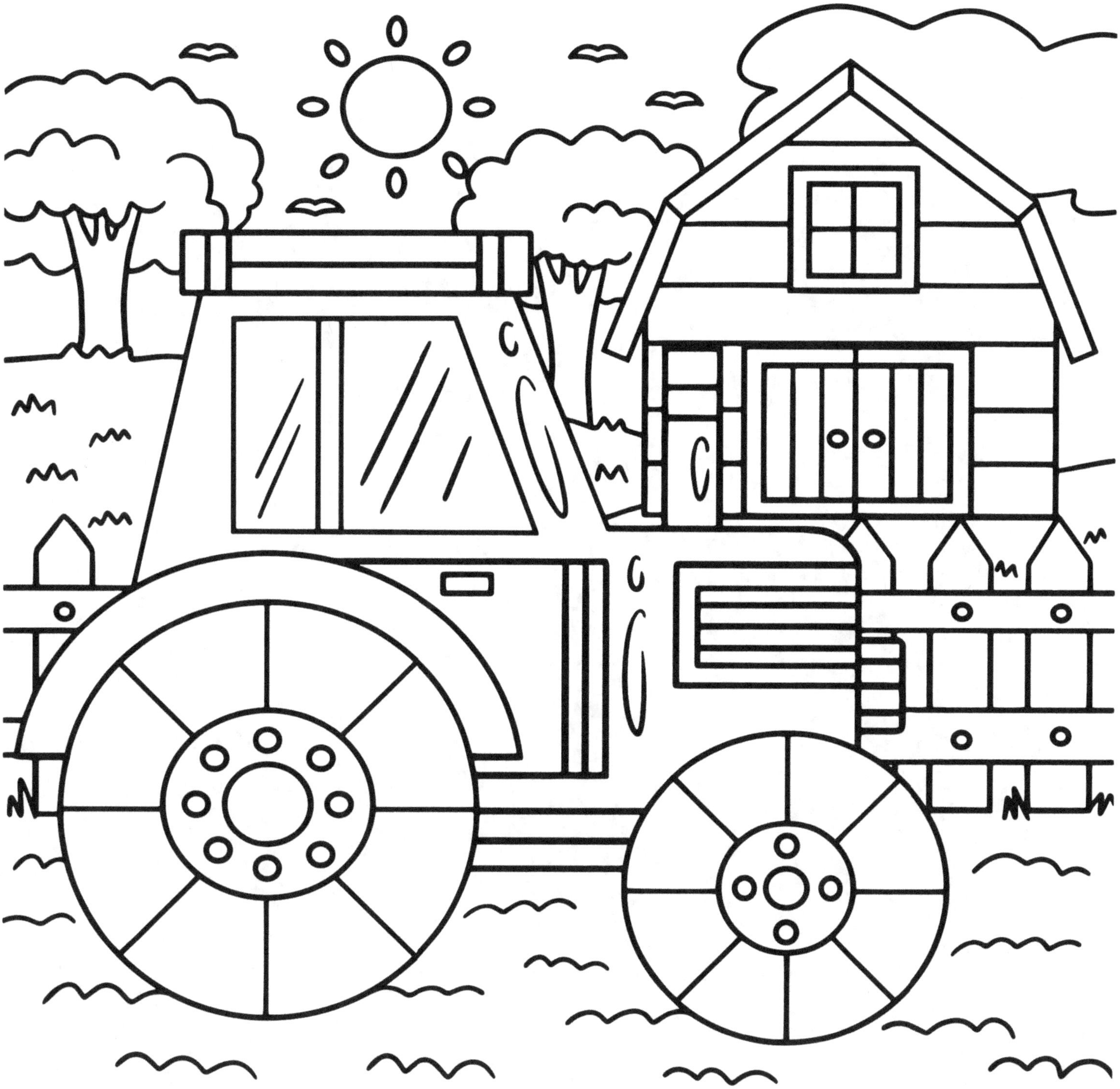

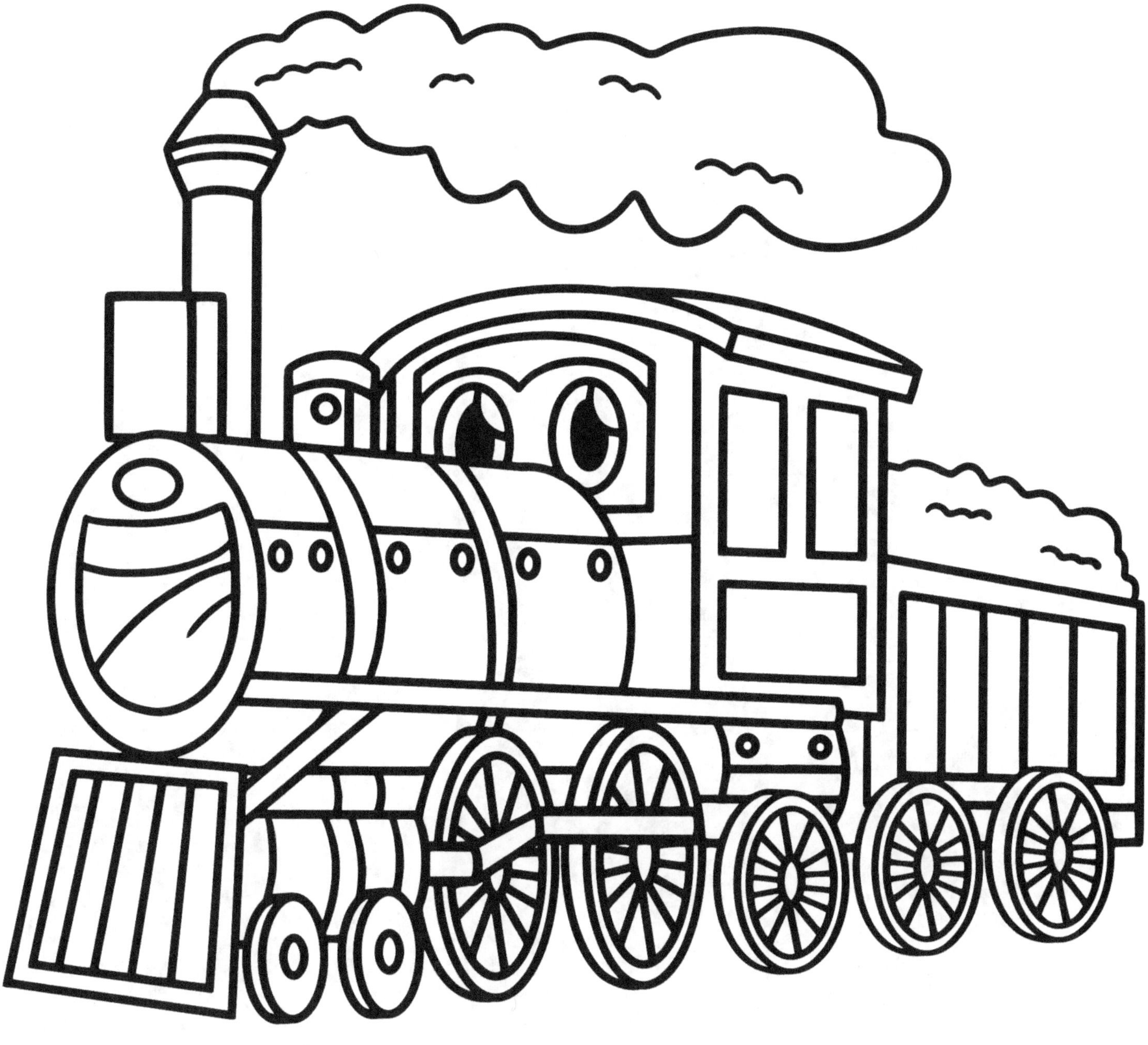

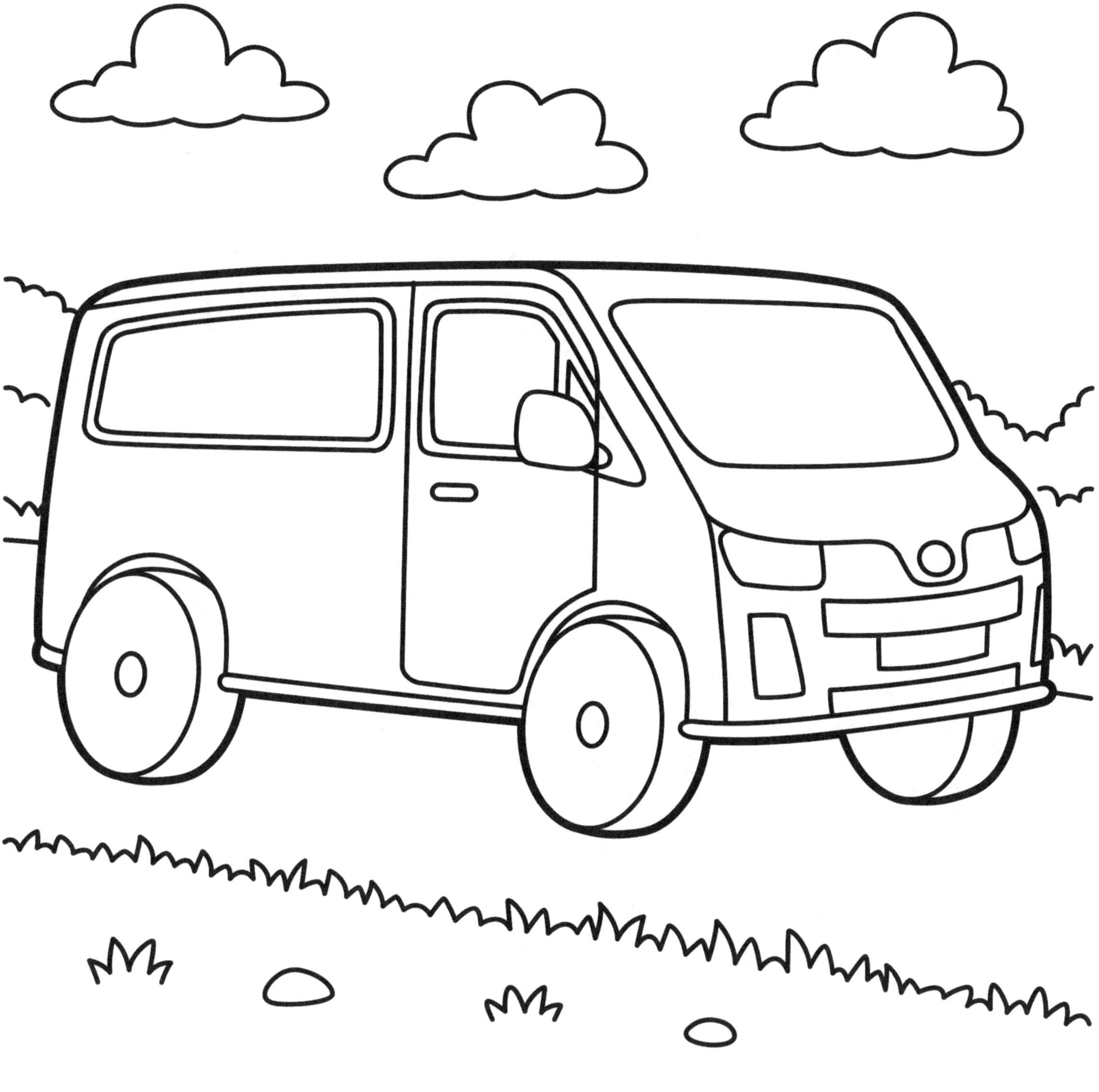

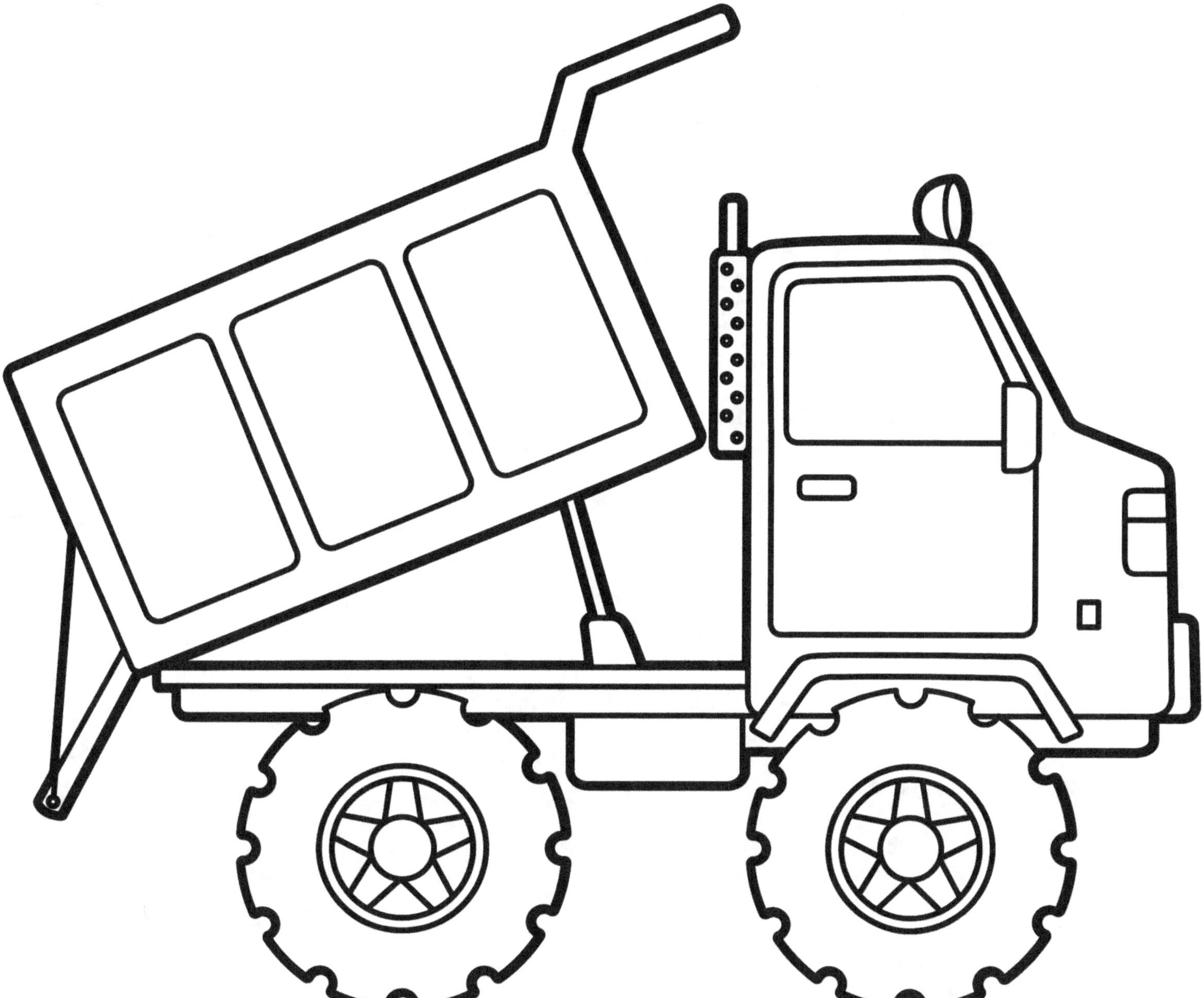

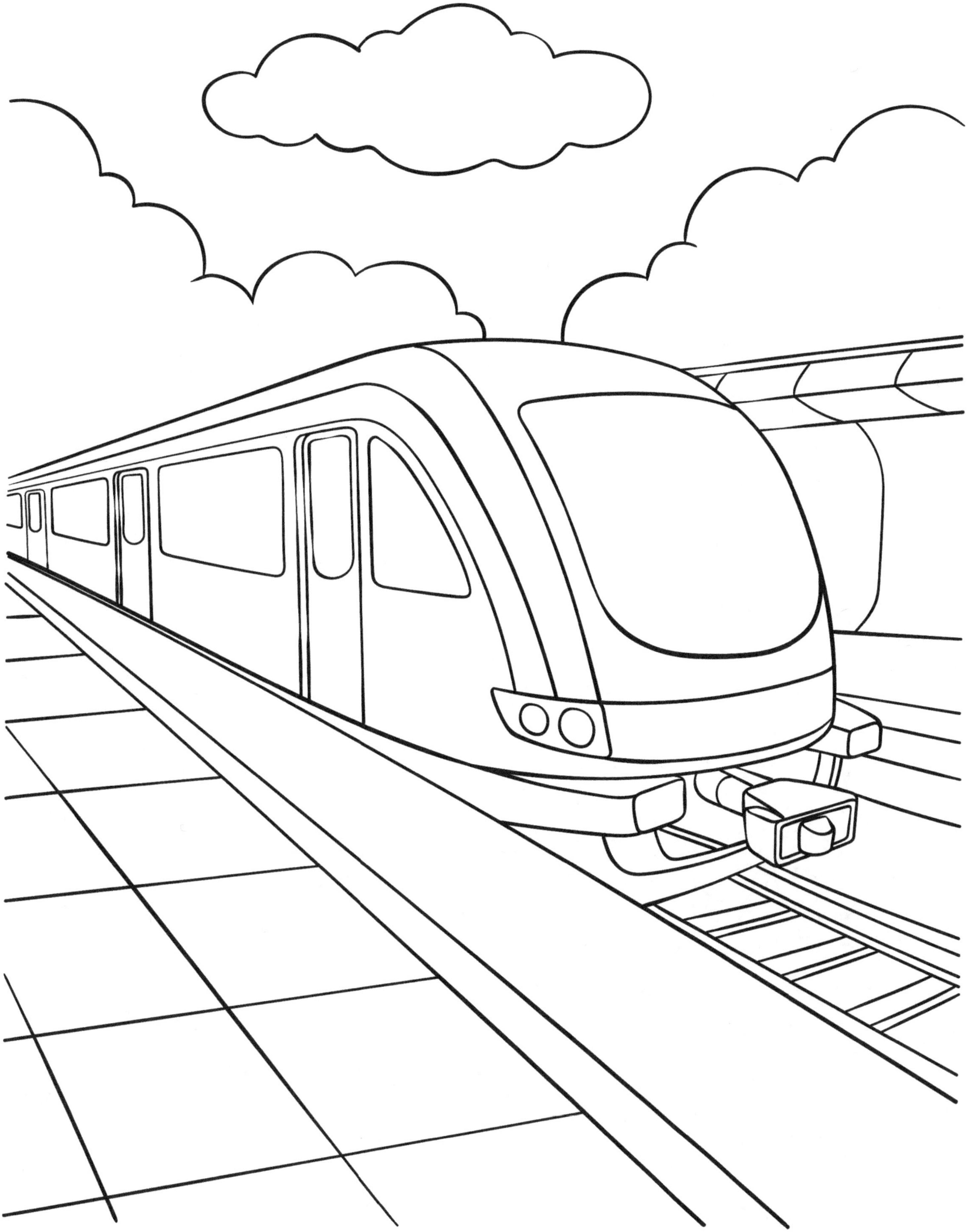

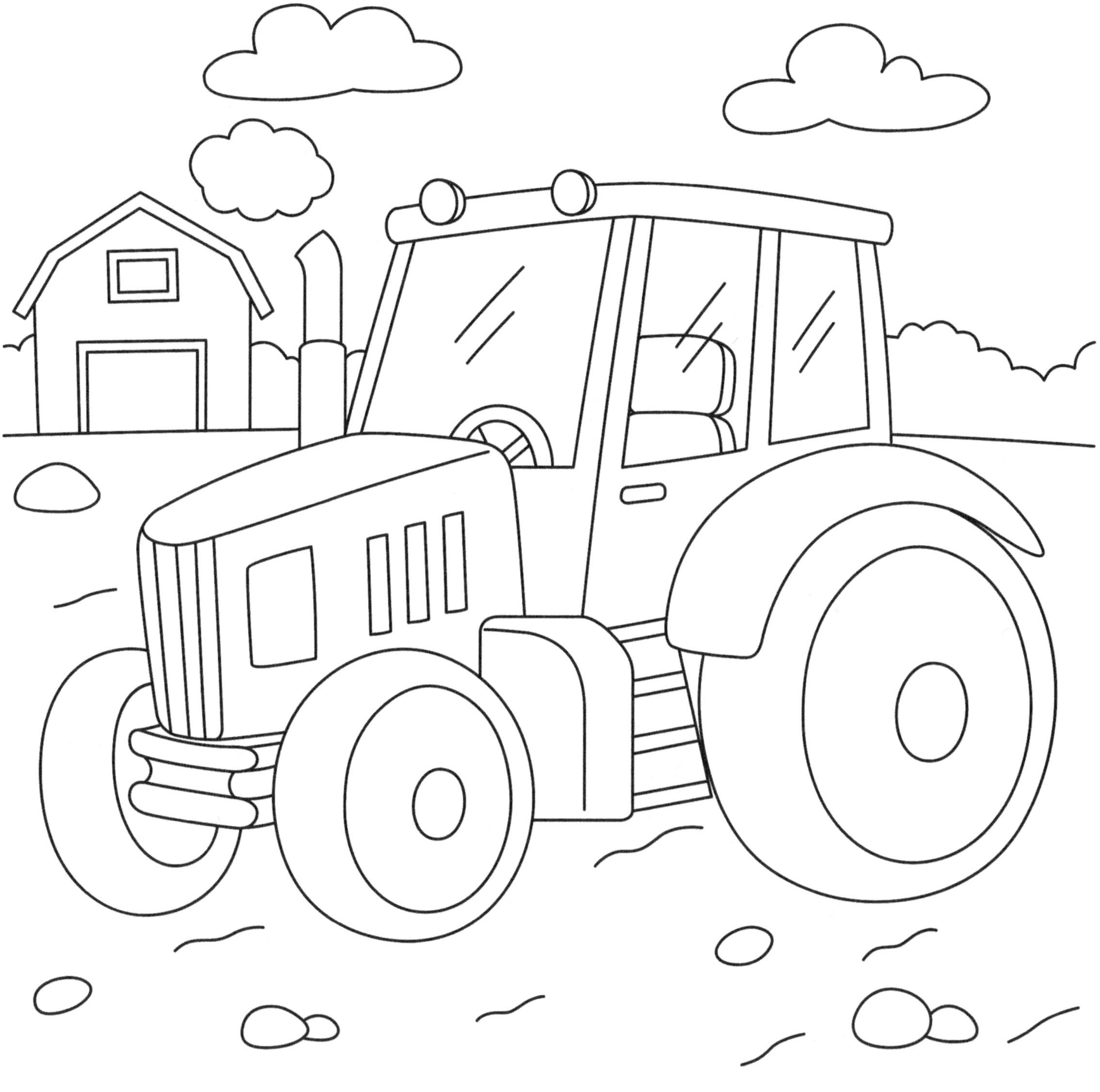

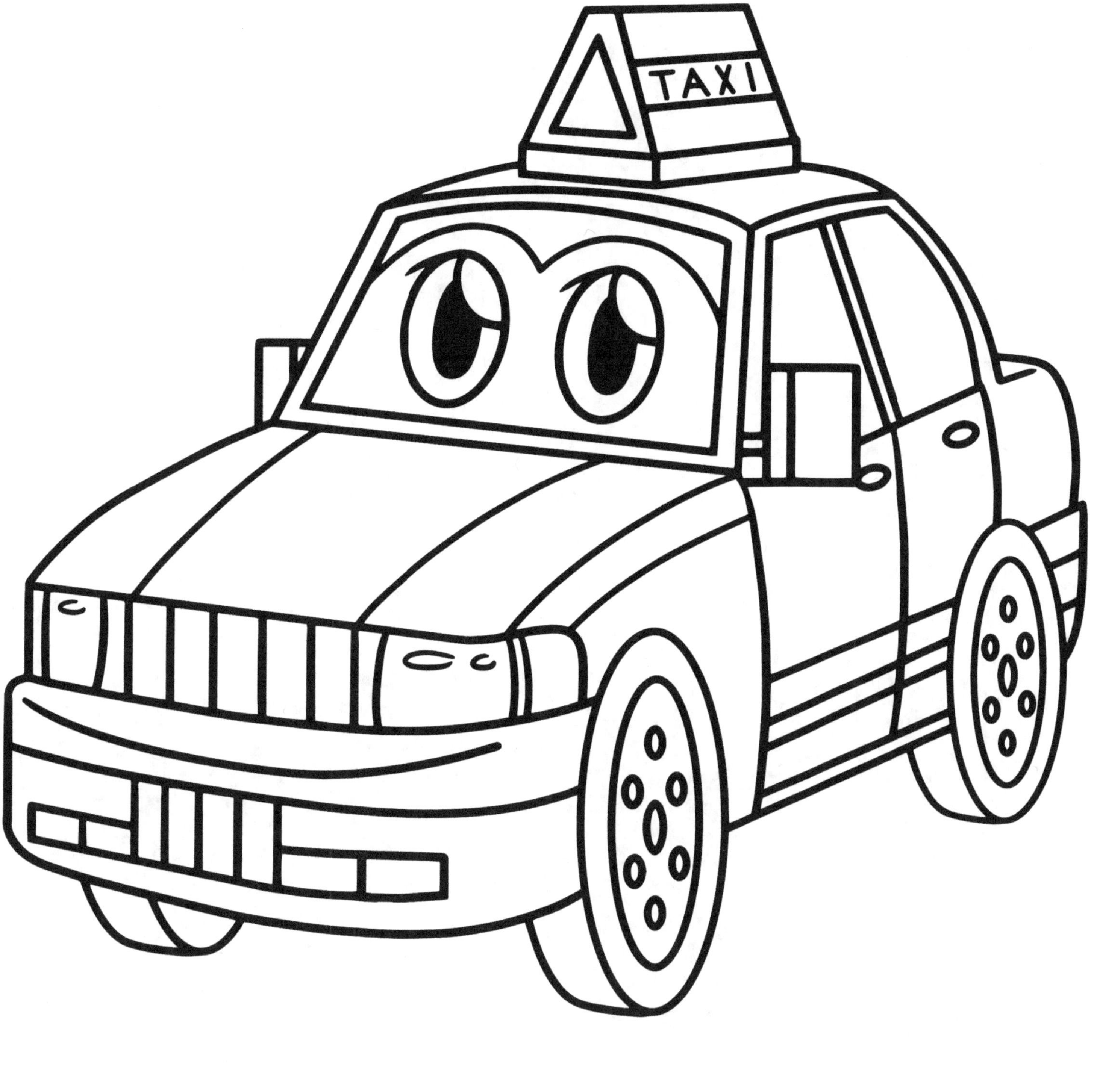
TAXI

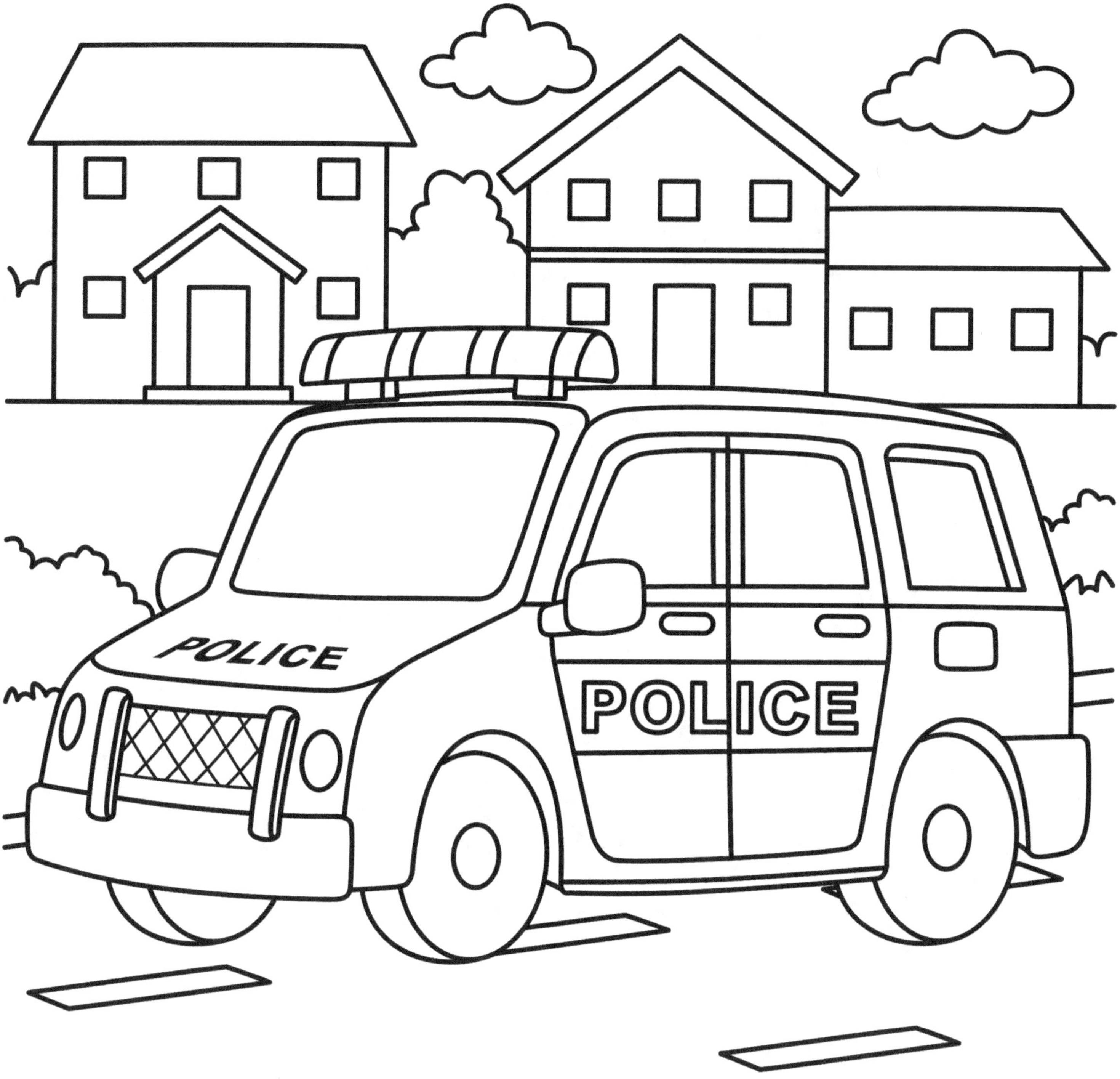
POLICE
POLICE

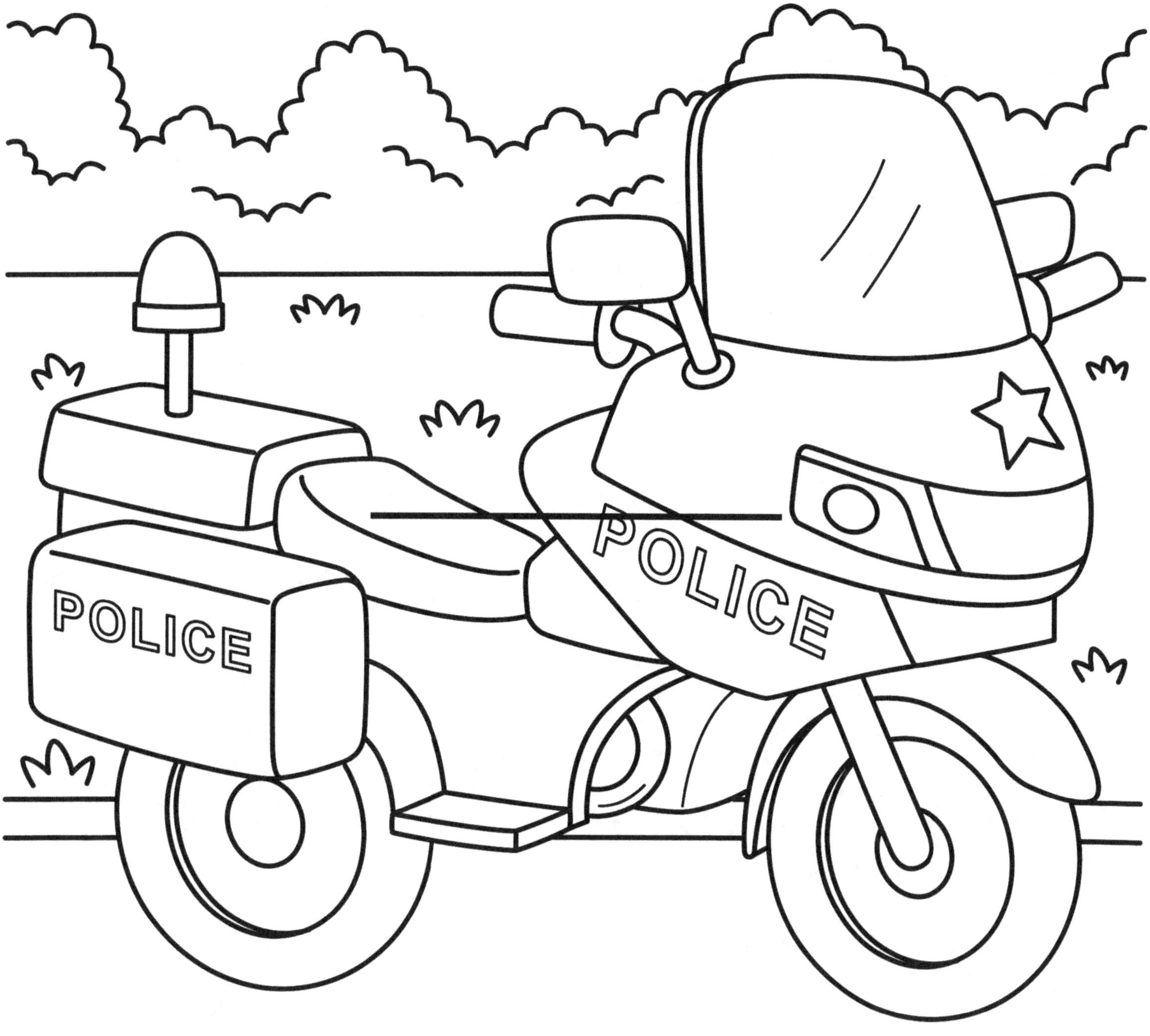
POLICE
POLICE

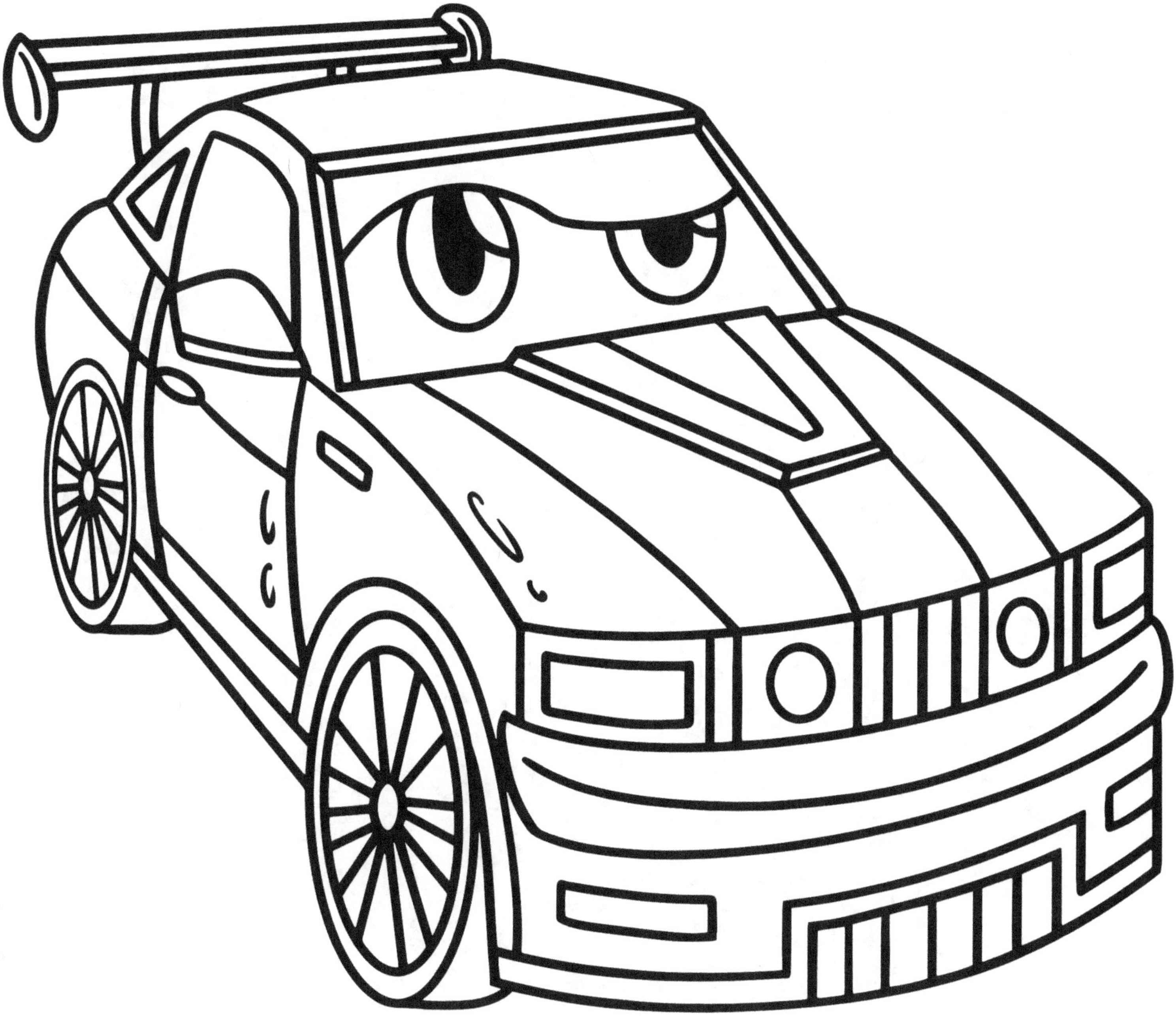

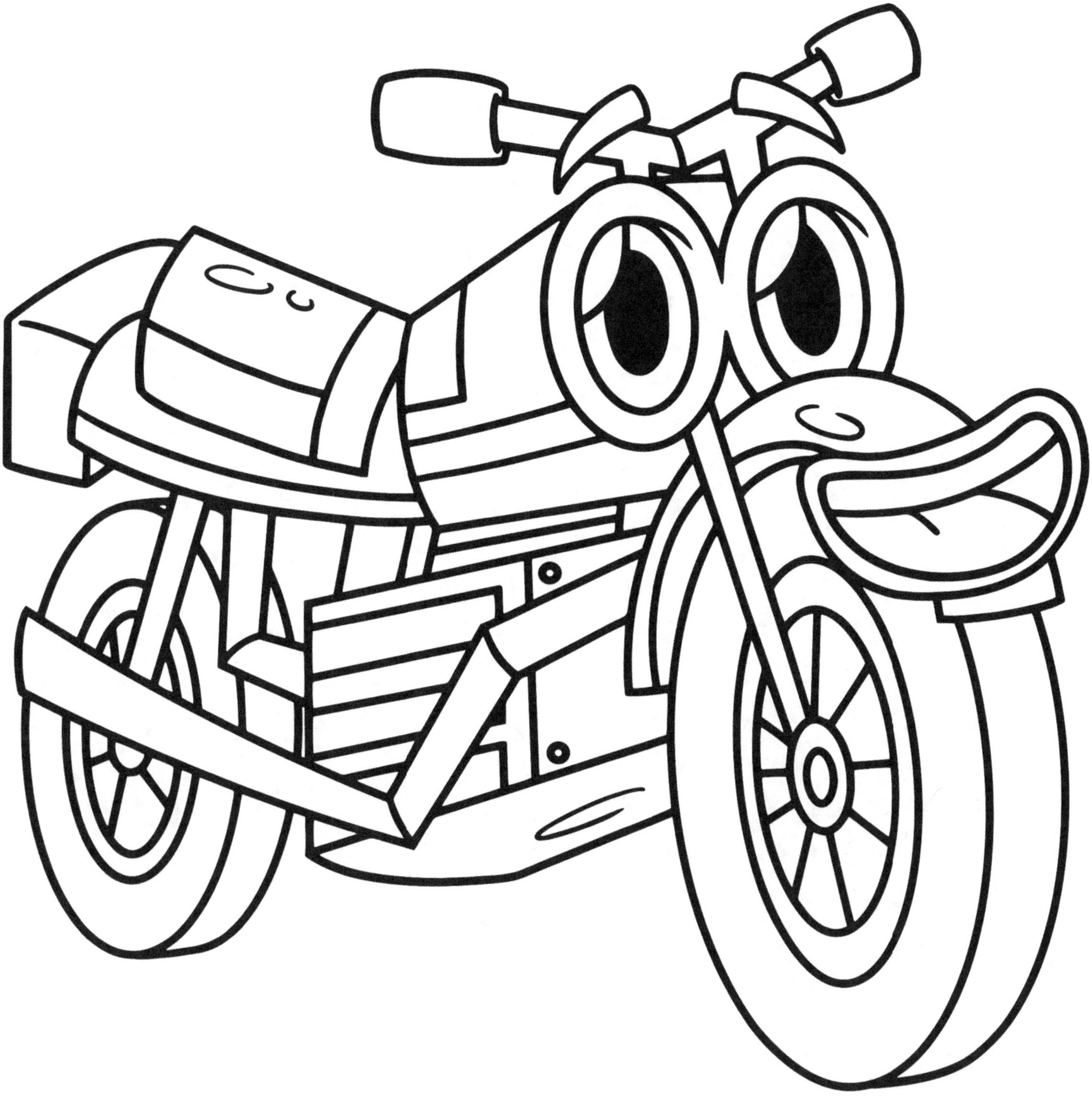

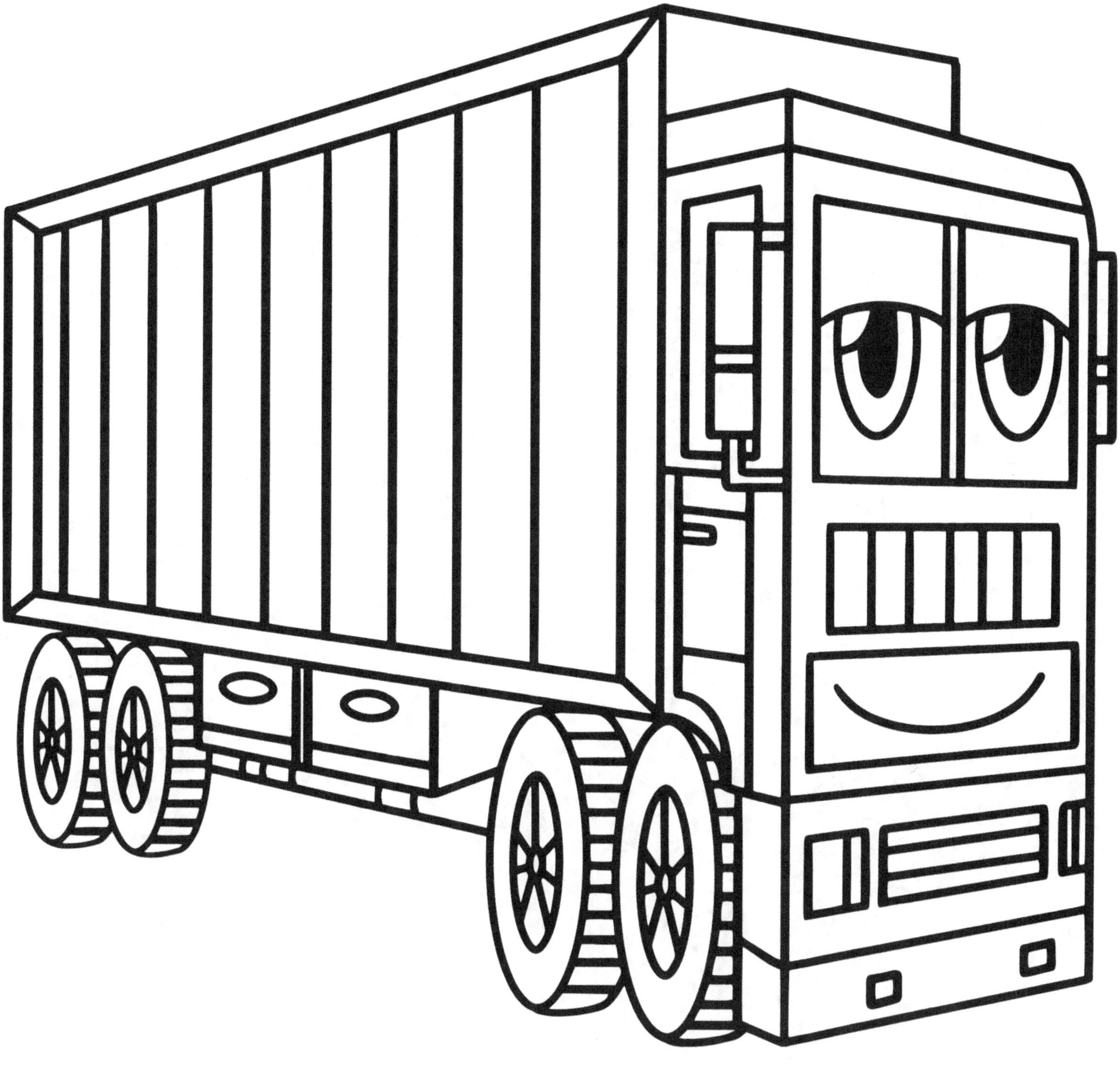

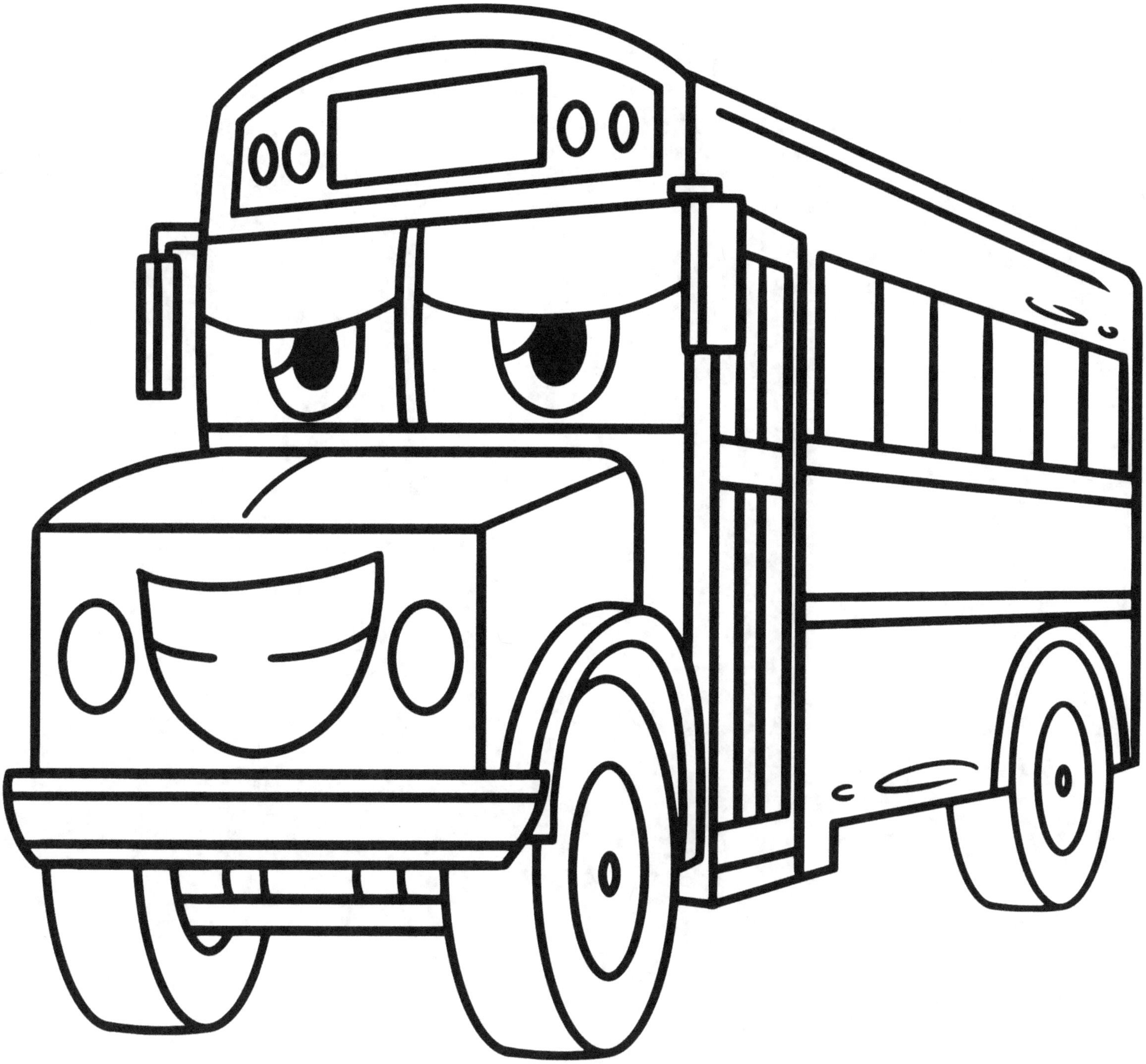

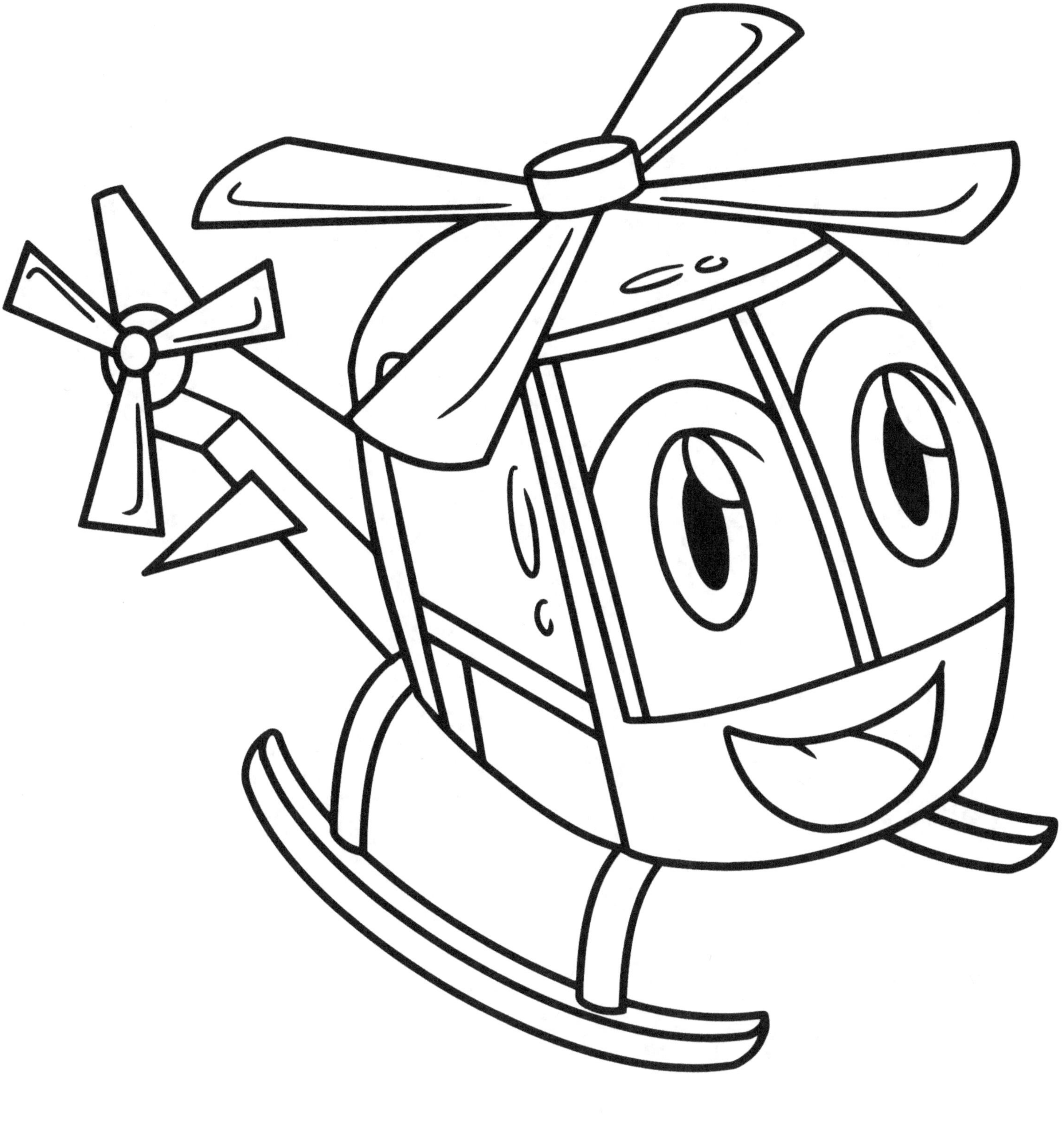

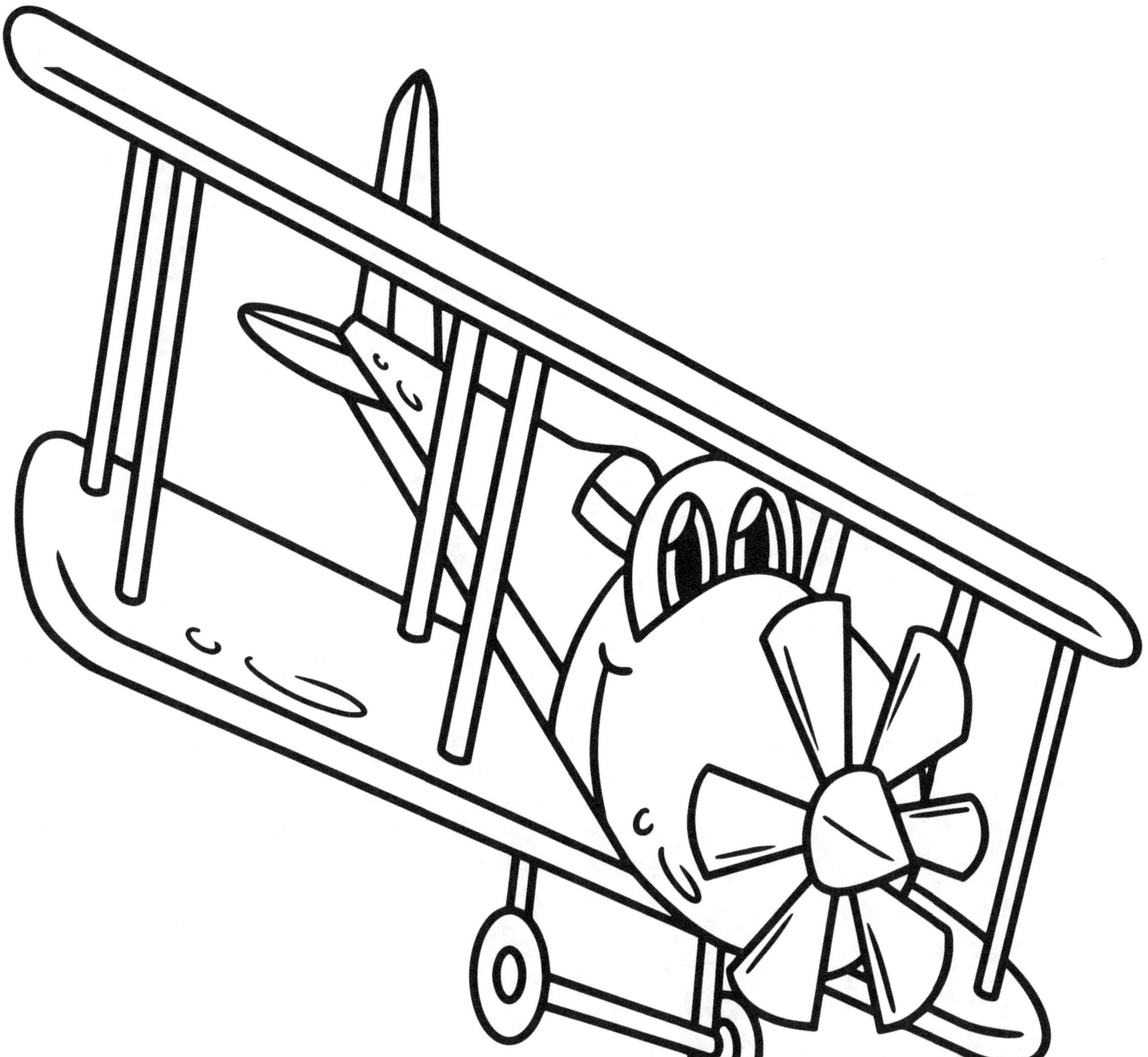

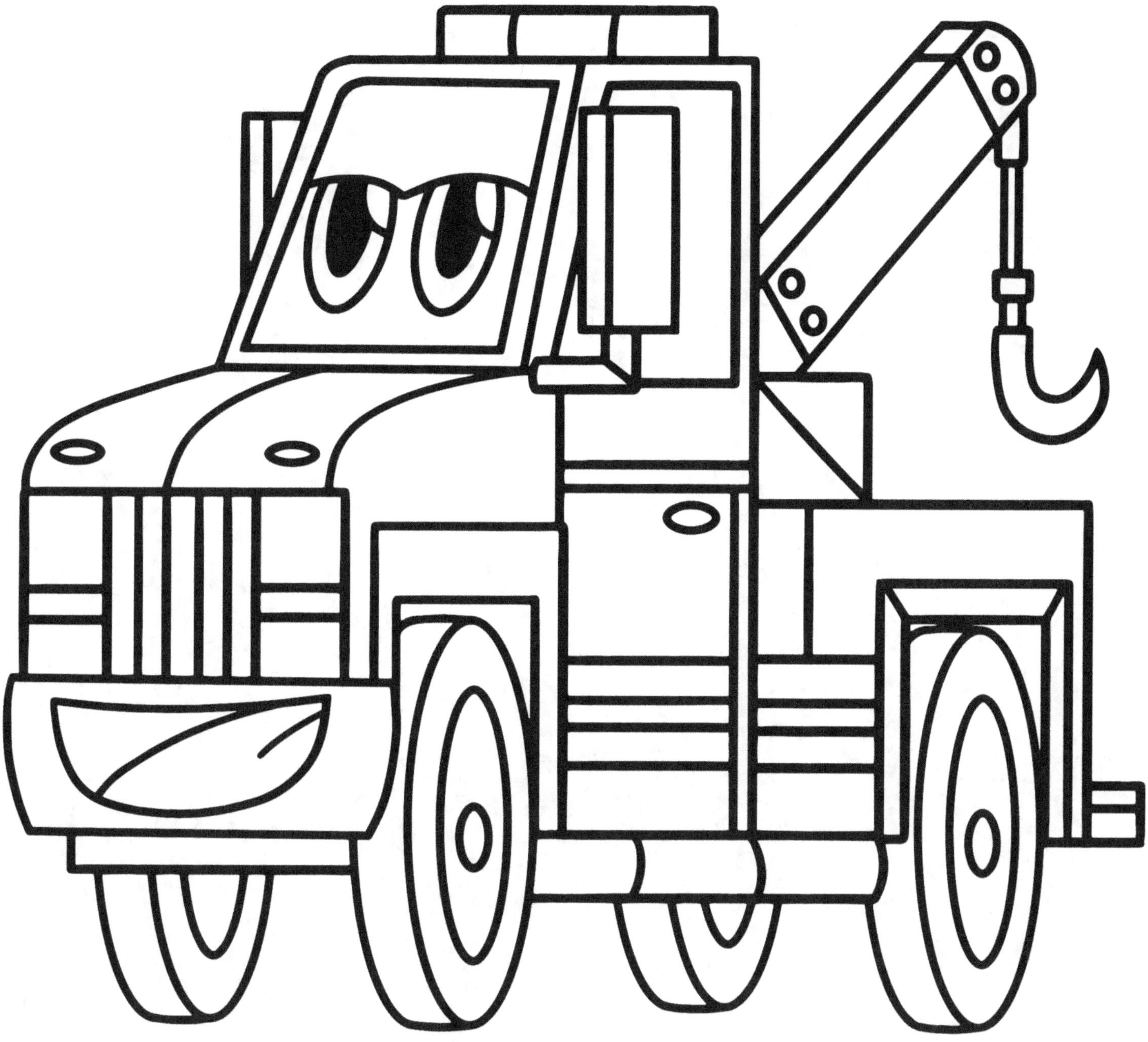

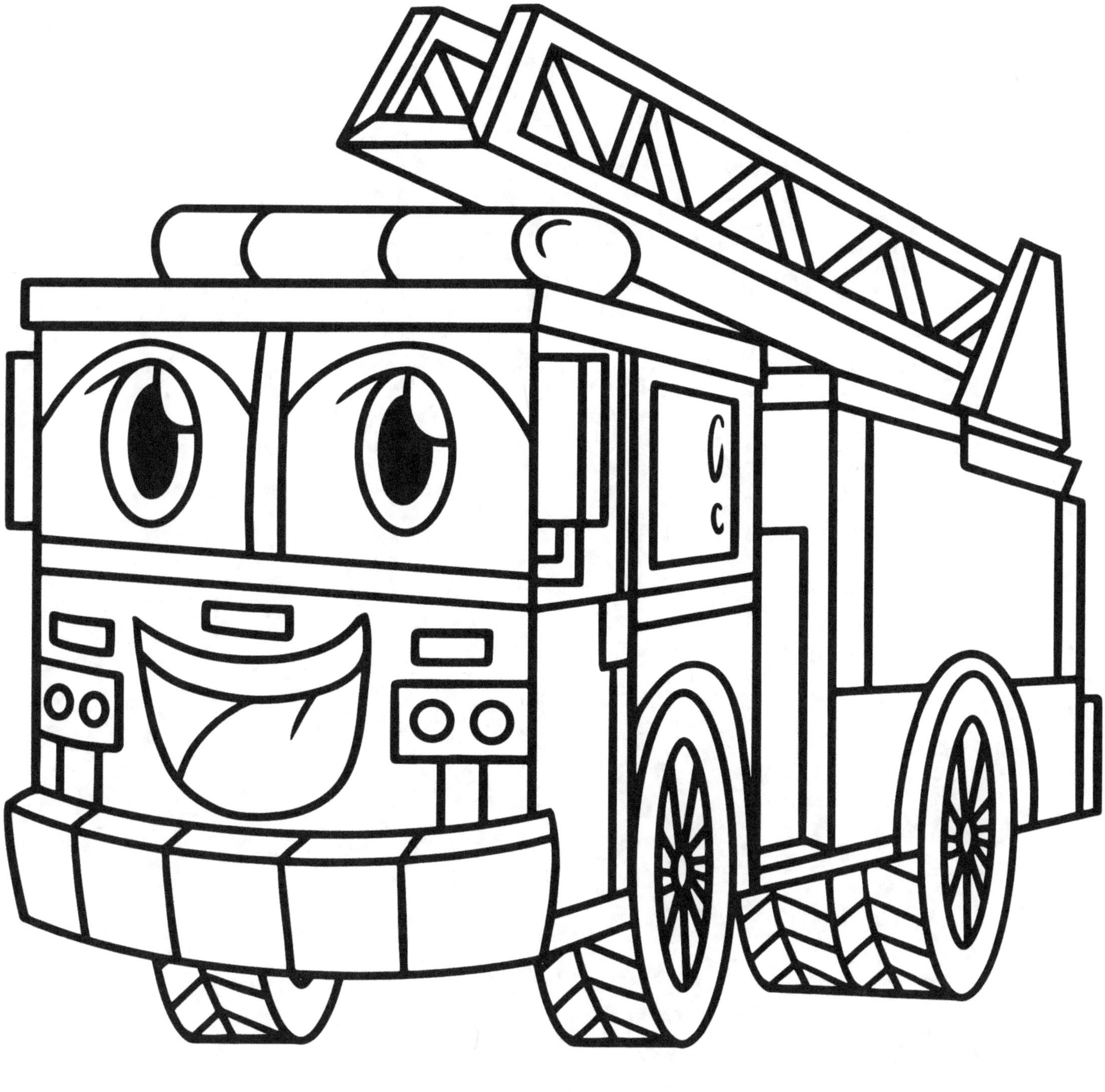

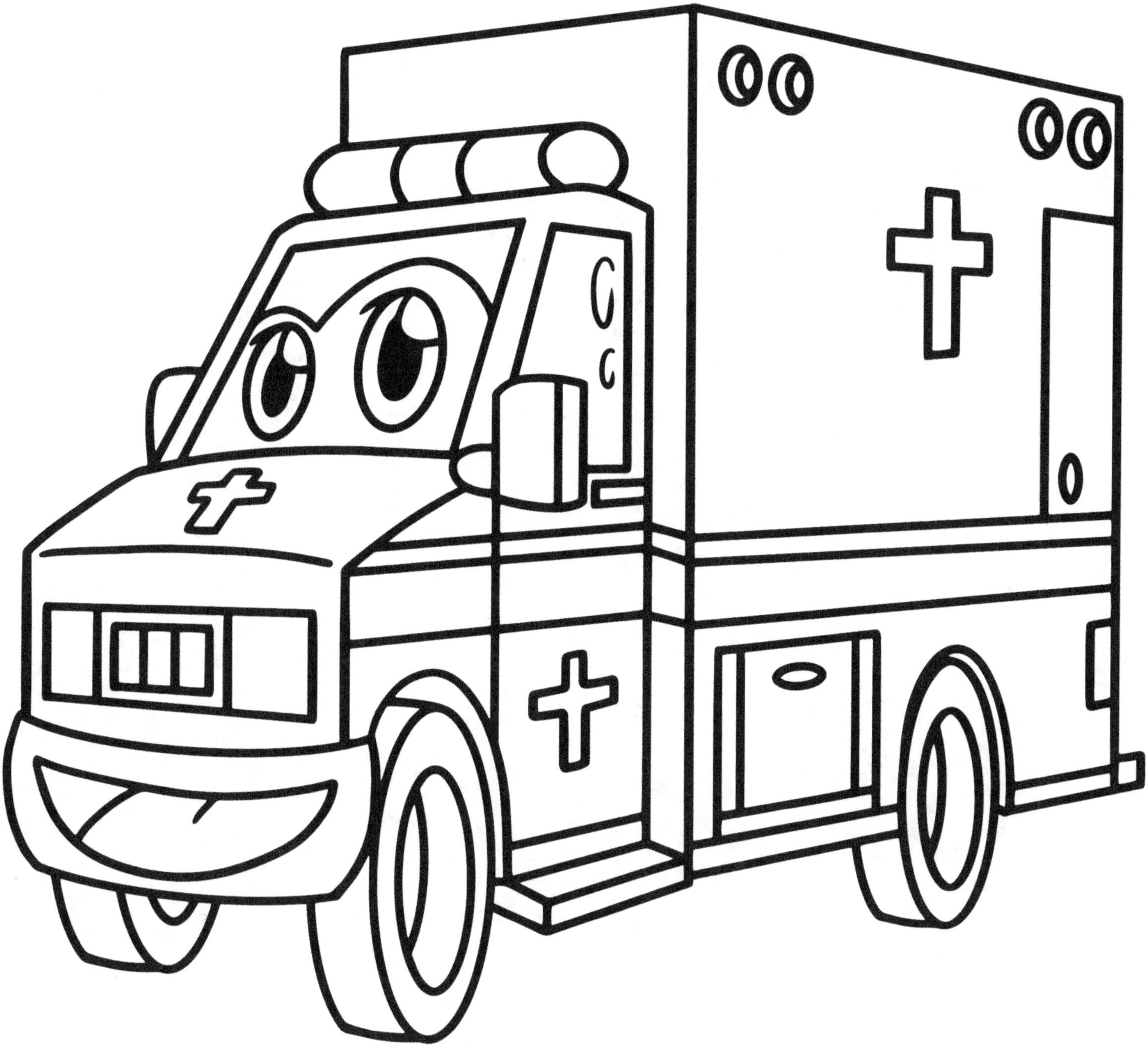

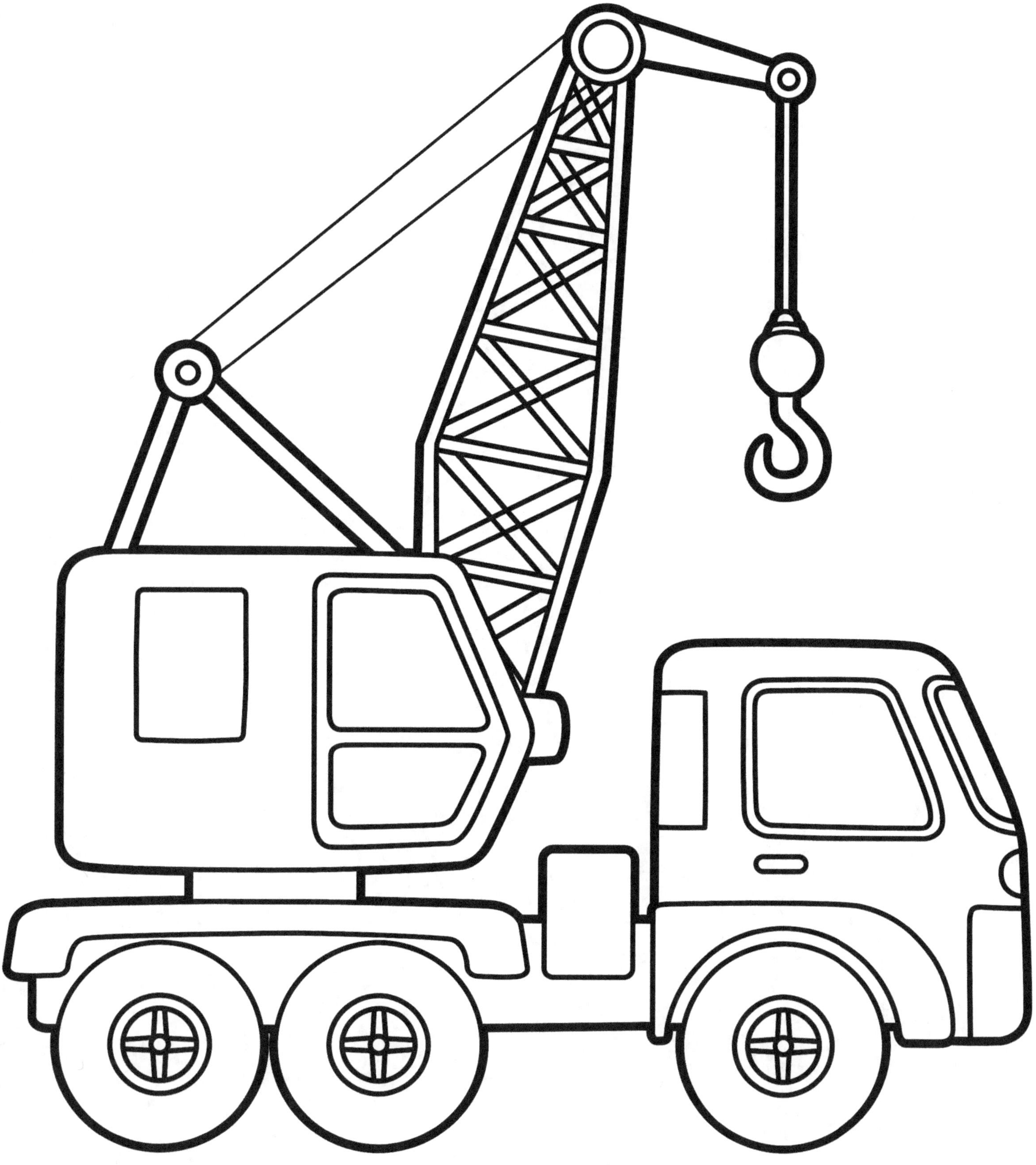

www.ingramcontent.com/pod-product-compliance
Lightning Source LLC
Chambersburg PA
CBHW081018240526
45471CB00017B/3413
* 9 7 9 8 3 2 1 3 4 2 2 2 0 *